YORK NOT

Silas Marner

George Eliot

Notes by Clare Findlay

Longman

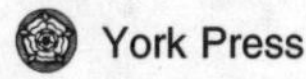

York Press

YORK PRESS
322 Old Brompton Road, London SW5 9JH

ADDISON WESLEY LONGMAN LIMITED
Edinburgh Gate, Harlow,
Essex CM20 2JE, United Kingdom
Associated companies, branches and representatives throughout the world.

First published 1997

ISBN 0–582–31472–0

Designed by Vicki Pacey, Trojan Horse
Illustrated by Kenny McKendry, Artist Partners
Map and Family Tree by Valerie Hill
Phototypeset by Gem Graphics, Trenance, Mawgan Porth, Cornwall
Produced by Longman Asia Limited, Hong Kong

Contents

PREFACE

York Notes are designed to give you a broader perspective on works of literature studied at GCSE and equivalent levels. We have carried out extensive research into the needs of the modern literature student prior to publishing this new edition. Our research showed that no existing series fully met students' requirements. Rather than present a single authoritative approach, we have provided alternative viewpoints, empowering students to reach their own interpretations of the text. York Notes provide a close examination of the work and include biographical and historical background, summaries, glossaries, analyses of characters, themes, structure and language, cultural connections and literary terms.

If you look at the Contents page you will see the structure for the series. However, there's no need to read from the beginning to the end as you would with a novel, play, poem or short story. Use the Notes in the way that suits you. Our aim is to help you with your understanding of the work, not to dictate how you should learn.

York Notes are written by English teachers and examiners, with an expert knowledge of the subject. They show you how to succeed in coursework and examination assignments, guiding you through the text and offering practical advice. Questions and comments will extend, test and reinforce your knowledge. Attractive colour design and illustrations improve clarity and understanding, making these Notes easy to use and handy for quick reference.

York Notes are ideal for:

- Essay writing
- Exam preparation
- Class discussion

The author of these Notes is Clare Findlay who gained a BA at Royal Holloway College, London University. She obtained a PGCE from Cambridge University and was the Head of English at St Anne's High School, Wolsingham, Co. Durham.

The text used in these Notes is the Penguin Classics Edition, 1996, edited by David Carroll.

Health Warning: **This study guide will enhance your understanding, but should not replace the reading of the original text and/or study in class.**

PART ONE

INTRODUCTION

HOW TO STUDY A NOVEL

You have bought this book because you wanted to study a novel on your own. This may supplement classwork.

- You will need to read the novel several times. Start by reading it quickly for pleasure, then read it slowly and carefully. Further readings will generate new ideas and help you to memorise the details of the story.
- Make careful notes on themes, plot and characters of the novel. The plot will change some of the characters. Who changes?
- The novel may not present events chronologically. Does the novel you are reading begin at the beginning of the story or does it contain flashbacks and a muddled time sequence? Can you think why?
- How is the story told? Is it narrated by one of the characters or by an all-seeing ('omniscient') narrator?
- Does the same person tell the story all the way through? Or do we see the events through the minds and feelings of a number of different people.
- Which characters does the narrator like? Which characters do you like or dislike? Do your sympathies change during the course of the book? Why? When?
- Any piece of writing (including your notes and essays) is the result of thousands of choices. No book had to be written in just one way: the author could have chosen other words, other phrases, other characters, other events. How could the author of your novel have written the story differently? If events were recounted by a minor character how would this change the novel?

Studying on your own requires self-discipline and a carefully thought-out work plan in order to be effective. Good luck.

GEORGE ELIOT'S BACKGROUND

George Eliot was born as Mary Ann Evans at Arbury Farm, Warwickshire, in 1819, to Robert Evans and his second wife, Christiana. She was the youngest of their three children and her father's favourite. He had two older children from his first wife.

This area was used in her description of Raveloe.

Shortly after Mary Ann's birth, the family moved to Griff House between Coventry and Nuneaton. Her father managed an estate in the rich farming countryside.

An unattractive child, Mary Ann was outstandingly clever, and devoted to her brother Isaac (born 1816). Their relationship was described in young Maggie Tulliver's love for her brother Tom in *The Mill on the Floss*.

Like Eppie, Mary Ann began her early education at a dame school. In 1824 she was sent away to school and was most unhappy. From 1828 in a school at Nuneaton, she excelled in music and at classical and modern languages. Her education was unusual for a girl at that time. She was greatly influenced by her teacher, Maria Lewis, whose strong evangelical and Calvinistic beliefs she enthusiastically adopted. These were described in the church at Lantern Yard.

This was similar to when Silas lost his faith.

By 1837 her mother was dead. Mary Ann had left school and was housekeeper to her father. Influenced by liberal free thinkers like Charles and Caroline Bray, whom she met after her move to Coventry in 1841, she had an extreme reaction to Christianity. Her father refused to speak to her until she agreed to behave respectably and attend church.

From 1844 she worked as a translator and by 1851 was unpaid assistant editor of a periodical *The Westminster Review*. Her father's death in 1849 had made her financially independent.

Through her publishing work she met many prominent

English, American and European writers. These included the lively G.H. Lewes who had separated from his wife. Legal conditions at that time prevented a divorce. He and Mary Ann (now Marian) caused a scandal, at first bringing social exclusion, by living together until his death in 1878. Her brother Isaac ended all family contact until she married J.W. Cross in 1880.

Silas Marner *grew from a childhood memory of a weaver with his bag.*

Persuaded by Lewes to write fiction, she was immediately successful. She published *Scenes from Clerical Life* in 1857 under the name of George Eliot. By using this male name, she hoped to protect her work and its sales from biased criticism because of her personal life and also from the dismissive attitude of the literary critics of the time towards female novelists. Like *Adam Bede* (1859), all her early books, including *Silas Marner* (1861), make use of her early life in Warwickshire to provide ideas and exact details of everyday country events.

George Eliot started *Romola* but interrupted it to write *Silas Marner*. Published in 1863, *Romola* was an historical novel set in fifteenth-century Florence. *Felix Holt* followed in 1866. This political novel was set in the changing England of the 1832 Parliamentary Reform Act – she had lived through this period herself as a child. *Middlemarch*, published 1872 but set in the same period as *Felix Holt*, was *A Study in Provincial Life*, according to its subtitle – again, this refers back to the countryside of her childhood. Regarded as George Eliot's best work, *Middlemarch* portrays the different interests and characters to be found in a small town and its surrounding countryside. Her last novel presented the Jewish *Daniel Deronda* (1876).

It is typical of all George Eliot's characters that they develop psychological insight into themselves and their moral position as they make their decisions.

CONTEXT & SETTING

An era of change

George Eliot began writing *Silas Marner* in autumn 1860. England was ending a century which had brought enormous changes in every area of life. Among the changes – there were many others – we find:

- The Industrial Revolution changed methods of production
- Factories were created
- The rise of great industrial towns
- A massive population shift
- Society changed from mainly agricultural to mainly industrial
- Attitudes about work, religion and government changed

The novel is striking for what it does not mention in its time span (c.1790–1820). Many major issues, including the following and many others, were ignored:

- The French Revolution and its effects
- The loss of America
- The abolition of the slave trade
- Catholic Emancipation
- Riots – from varied causes
- Many repressive laws – including suspension of Habeas Corpus and the Anti-Combination Acts
- India

The Napoleonic Wars (1793–1815) against France had widespread effects but only one is mentioned in *Silas Marner* – the economic effect on farming.

- Eppie came to Silas during 'that glorious war-time' (p. 23) when the high price of food made farmers rich.
- She marries when peace has brought the 'increasing poor rate' and 'ruinous times' (p. 151) which upset Mr Lammeter and Godfrey.

Another topical cause of great unrest, urban social conditions, is mentioned in Chapter 21 when Silas and

George Eliot recreated 'old-fashioned village life' to contrast industrial values and conditions.

Eppie try to visit Lantern Yard. The vast changes brought by the Industrial Revolution caused hardship to many and led to riots. The hardship is hinted in the description of the 'great manufacturing town' (p. 177) and a 'dark ugly place' (p. 178). Indeed, Eppie can hardly believe 'any folks lived i' this way, so close together' (p. 178).

Before the opening of the novel (c.1800) Silas had worked in the town which he is unable to recognise thirty years later; so he stops 'several persons in succession' (p. 178) to check its name.

The contrast with the pleasantly situated and 'important-looking' (p. 7) village of Raveloe, with its closely knit and cooperative community, is shown by Eppie's 'distress' when she visits Lantern Yard. She is 'ill at ease' with the 'multitude of strange indifferent faces' (p. 178). The people are not interested in strangers. Unlike Raveloe, there is little curiosity in people or events.

Silas feels ill with shock that Lantern Yard has been replaced by 'a large factory' (p. 179), but the brush-maker arrived 'only ten years ago' (p. 179) and cannot help with information.

Why is setting important?

Setting is often vital to a novel's plot or action. National and international events influence the lives, thoughts, attitudes and actions of people living through them. The book's characters live inside its action or plot and are affected by the existing mental and physical conditions of their period and place.

The setting makes boundaries for the story. Look for the clues which create:

- The historical date or period when the story happens
- Where the events happen

Silas Marner is set in the countryside and in a village community almost untouched by events elsewhere. The effects of the Industrial Revolution do not affect Silas until he is 'Fifty-five, as near as I can say' (p. 167), when 'the weaving was going down' (p. 141) following the spread of the powered loom, invented by Cartwright in 1794.

Always make full use of details provided by the author.

George Eliot works hard on the details of her settings so that you can imagine or visualise people and events. For example, Raveloe lay 'in a rich central plain … nestled in a snug well-wooded hollow quite an hour's journey on horseback from any turnpike' (p. 7). It is 'important-looking', had 'two or three large brick-and-stone homesteads … standing close on the road' and has 'well-walled orchards and ornamental weathercocks' (p. 7). Such detail gives us Raveloe's geographical position, atmosphere and period.

Raveloe was typical of any village before the Industrial Revolution. Its class structure is shown through;

- Village customs and leisure – the Rainbow, Christmas and New Year parties
- Travel – gentry and other people
- Dress – gentry and others – notice how details reveal class
- Religion: town – chapel, artisan class, Calvin / Wesley; country – church, Rector (Mr Crackenthorpe), Parish clerk (Mr Macey), Deputy (Mr Tookey) and others

Social class is based on housing (compare Red House and Silas's cottage), land ownership, work (compare town and country trades and the difference between Squire Cass and the other farmers), health and social care and education.

Make your own lists – quote to prove points you make.

As you read *Silas Marner*, try to keep notes on these topics – it will make your essay writing and revision for any examination much easier.

Part two

Summaries

General summary

Chapters 1–3 Around 1805, the linen-weaver Silas Marner moves to a cottage outside Raveloe. He works long hours and is antisocial. The villagers' fear of Silas increases and, after helping Sally Oates, he refuses to aid anyone through his herbal knowledge.

Raveloe is a very different world from the northern town where Silas had grown up and belonged to a strict religious group. Silas suffers from fits and his friend, William Dane, had taken advantage of this to frame Silas for theft. Silas was expelled from his church. His fiancée, Sarah, ended their engagement and had married William.

Squire Cass is a bad father and landlord. His oldest son, Godfrey, is blackmailed into giving his tenant's rent to Dunstan – the Squire's second son. Dunstan threatens to tell the Squire of Godfrey's secret marriage to Molly Farren, and refuses to repay the rent. He persuades Godfrey to sell Wildfire – his horse.

Chapters 4–10 Before Dunstan can sell Wildfire, the horse dies during a hunt. As Dunstan walks home, he sees Silas's cottage and decides to 'borrow' the weaver's gold. The cottage is empty, and quickly finding the hidden gold, Dunstan steals it and disappears.

Silas discovers his beloved gold is missing and rushes to the Rainbow for help. Meanwhile, uninterested in the missing Dunstan, the Squire urges Godfrey to propose to Nancy Lammeter.

Silas's misery changes the villagers' attitude to him. Among others, Dolly Winthrop visits and invites Silas to church.

Chapters 11–15 Molly Farren's revenge on Godfrey is to present their child to the Squire at his New Year's Eve party.

An opium addict, she collapses in the snow and dies near Silas's cottage. The child enters his cottage and Silas mistakes her hair for his returned gold. He finds the collapsed Molly and goes to fetch Dr Kimble from the party. Godfrey recognises his daughter in Silas's arms but keeps silent.

Eppie changes Silas's life and character. He regains trust in God and humanity through Eppie's personality and the interest of the admiring villagers.

Chapters 16–18 Godfrey marries Nancy but after sixteen years they are childless. He wants to adopt Eppie but Nancy believes adoption is wrong. Dunstan's body is discovered in the quarry with Silas's gold. Godfrey tells Nancy that Molly Farren was his wife and that Eppie is his daughter. Unexpectedly, Nancy forgives him and they agree to adopt Eppie. Neither considers Silas.

Chapter 19 – Conclusion Godfrey apologises to Silas for Dunstan's theft. He offers to adopt Eppie – who refuses. Godfrey reveals he is Eppie's birth father; twice more, supported by Nancy, he offers to adopt Eppie. Twice Silas tells Eppie to consider her future. She turns the offers down. She chooses to stay with Silas and marry Aaron Winthrop. At their wedding, Mr Macey voices the feelings of everyone – Silas has won the respect and admiration of all through his own actions.

DETAILED SUMMARIES

CHAPTER 1

Silas Marner lives and works as a weaver outside the village of Raveloe. It is about 1805 and, when the novel opens, he has been there for fifteen years. It is a remote village where everyone is suspicious of newcomers – especially when they do an unusual job like weaving and have an unfortunate appearance. Silas chooses to live alone and at a distance from people.

This is because fifteen years earlier he had been falsely accused of theft by his best friend, William Dane. Church money had been stolen from the house of a dying member of the strict Christian group, meeting in Lantern Yard, to which they both belonged.

William, a young weaver of about Silas's age, had become jealous of Silas for two reasons. Firstly, Sarah – the servant to whom Silas was engaged; and secondly, the respect given to Silas by other members of their religious group because of his good life and fits. Silas suffered from cataleptic fits; he went rigid and into a kind of trance but remained upright. He had had one of these fits as he watched over a dying leader of the church. William, who should have watched later, had seized his chance to steal the money. He accused Silas of theft and later married Sarah himself.

William had planted evidence against Silas in his room and managed to fix the drawing of lots which 'proved' Silas guilty and expelled him from the church.

Look for other ways in which Silas is different.

Silas then decided that God could not exist, and, after his move to Raveloe, he lives only for his work and the money it brings. His continued unfriendliness and his refusal to help others with herbal cures (apart from Sally Oates) combine to keep the superstitious villagers continually distant and afraid, despite Silas's growing wealth.

COMMENT

The first page of the novel takes us back to early-nineteenth-century England (c.1800–5) before the changes of the Industrial Revolution. We read descriptions of activities, people and ideas that were already old-fashioned in 1861 – when the book was first published.

The author's style in the opening is important. Think about how George Eliot creates the slow pace of time and allows us to see Raveloe and its surrounding countryside.

We meet the main character, Silas Marner, and learn that his work as a weaver makes him different from the farming community. An important theme is introduced; that he is an outsider. We discover several other ways in which he differs from the villagers, including his appearance.

Look to see where and how the false accusation he suffers is later reflected by his accusation against another innocent person.

We learn that the villagers avoid or fear Silas for various reasons. Some of these are not of Silas's making, but result from Raveloe's isolated position. The villagers' old-fashioned, superstitious beliefs have not yet been changed by new ideas and inventions. The author tells us through a flashback that Silas was once very different. His earlier trusting and generous personality is contrasted with his present character.

A sense of community or belonging is a key idea in this book. Look at the early similarities between Silas and William Dane in their religious group. Think about the ways a real Christian should behave in these circumstances. Compare this with the community's treatment of Silas.

GLOSSARY

chary of his time avoided wasting time
Evil One the devil
winnowing machine/flail modern (1881) and old methods of separating harvested corn from its chaff
those war times 1793–1815 Napoleonic wars enriched farmers
on the parish a tax used to support the very poor at home or in the workhouse
Assurance of salvation Calvin's teaching promised heaven to souls chosen by God
calling and election sure another reference to Calvin's teaching
cataleptic fit a form of fit – the sufferer goes rigid
praying and drawing lots a method used by early Christians to make decisions

CHAPTER 2

Look for three ways in which Silas's past experience influences his life in Raveloe.

Alone, over fifteen years, Silas has become obsessed with work and is a miser. He looks and behaves in an increasingly odd manner. His gold has become his hobby and has replaced friends. Raveloe is described and is as different from Lantern Yard as if it were a foreign country.

To avoid his painful memories, Silas works at his household tasks and at his weaving 'like a spinning insect'. He now needs little money as he no longer gives to the church. He increasingly enjoys seeing and touching his gold, which he keeps in leather bags in the floor under his loom.

After helping Sally Oates's heart problem, his refusal of his herbal medicines to other villagers increases their suspicion and dislike.

COMMENT

The simple, plain chapel and strict narrow beliefs of Silas's earlier life as an evangelical Christian in a northern town make Raveloe seem like a foreign country because its inhabitants are easy about religion and live in comfortable plenty.

Losing his spiritual life is a disaster to Silas who copes by spending hours mechanically weaving. The weaving changes Silas's personality. His aim is now the gold itself instead of what the money could buy.

The author gives the villagers a collective voice as they discuss and hold general opinions. Silas 'came from nobody knew where'. Throughout the book, look for their opinions on events and individuals.

Note the irony (see Literary Terms) that Silas hides his gold. Because of the setting (c.1805) Silas does not expect to be robbed, yet he hides his gold – and is robbed! The villagers know each other so well that robbers are rare. To enjoy his loot, a robber would have to leave the village which is his whole world: 'a course as dark and dubious as a balloon journey'.

GLOSSARY

Lethean from Lethe, the river of forgetfulness in Greek mythology
amulet a magic charm protecting the wearer
native (gods) belonging to the area / locality one comes from
Power God / the supernatural
Unseen Love God / the supernatural

CHAPTER 3

Squire Cass is the largest landowner in Raveloe, although others, like Mr Osgood, are nearly his equal. As food producers, the farmers gain from the high food prices caused by the Napoleonic wars. They enjoy the easier winter months, visiting each other and holding parties. The villagers approve of this lifestyle, as by custom they receive the leftovers. They disapprove, however, of the squire's upbringing of his sons after his wife had died and of their resulting characters. They hope the oldest, Godfrey, will rescue his family by marrying Nancy Lammeter, the capable and attractive daughter of a greatly respected neighbouring farmer. They greatly dislike his second son, Dunstan, known as Dunsey.

Fifteen years after Silas moved to Raveloe, we meet the Cass brothers quarrelling on a dark November afternoon in their uncomfortable home – both have been drinking. Godfrey demands the return of money belonging to his father, the rent from a man called Fowler. His father believes that Fowler has not paid the rent, and says that he will order Fowler's possessions to be seized. Godfrey had lent the money to Dunstan who now refuses to repay it. Dunsey threatens to have Godfrey disinherited by revealing his marriage to Molly Farren, once a pretty barmaid.

Godfrey becomes so desperate that he considers telling his father the truth. This would make the Squire throw out both his sons. However, after Godfrey has considered this possibility, he decides to take up Dunstan's offer to sell Wildfire, his horse and the only valuable thing he owns.

How do the inhabitants of Raveloe view the Cass family?

Godfrey is unable to attend the hunt on the following day because he plans to go to Mrs Osgood's birthday dance where he hopes to meet Nancy. He wishes also to avoid Batherley, where the hunt will meet, because Molly Farren lives there. Most reluctantly he agrees Dunstan will go in his place and sell the horse.

Comment

We meet members of the small landowner class, who are often called 'the gentry' because they either own or rent their farms. The title of 'Squire', already old-fashioned elsewhere, is given to Mr Cass because he owns the most land in Raveloe.

We begin to learn of the social structure of Raveloe. Careful reading of Chapter 3 gives details of the characters and daily lives of Squire Cass and his two oldest sons. It also reveals village opinion on them. Class divisions are very important in this book.

The villagers consider Squire Cass a bad father, another key theme in the book. Their clear opinions on the two oldest sons comes just before we judge them for ourselves.

Godfrey has problems in addition to the money. He loves and, off and on, has been openly courting Nancy Lammeter. However, his marriage to Molly, to whom he once had been passionately attracted, is a secret. Molly's lower social class would make her unacceptable to the proud squire. In any case Godfrey has tired of her, her drunkenness, her drugs and her demands for money. Godfrey's situation allows Dunstan to blackmail him for money. We are told the reasons why Godfrey married Molly Farren whom he now increasingly hates. In contrast, he sees Nancy as the ideal wife he has lost through his own faults.

GLOSSARY

orts dialect word (see Literary Terms) for leftovers, traditionally given to the poor
pillions second seat behind horserider to carry passenger
chines name for a meat joint
King George George III, reigned 1760–1820
foxes' brushes trophies made from the tails resulting from a successful hunt
cut off with a shilling a metaphor for being disinherited
laudanum legal pain-killing liquid made from opium
sword hanging over him an allusion (see Literary Terms) to a sword hanging by a thread above the head of Damocles
crooked sixpence a traditional good luck symbol
rioting a rollicking lifestyle
like demons in a ready-garnished home an allusion to New Testament Luke 11: efforts to remedy a bad situation produce a worse situation

TEST YOURSELF (Chapters 1–3)

A *Identify the speaker.*

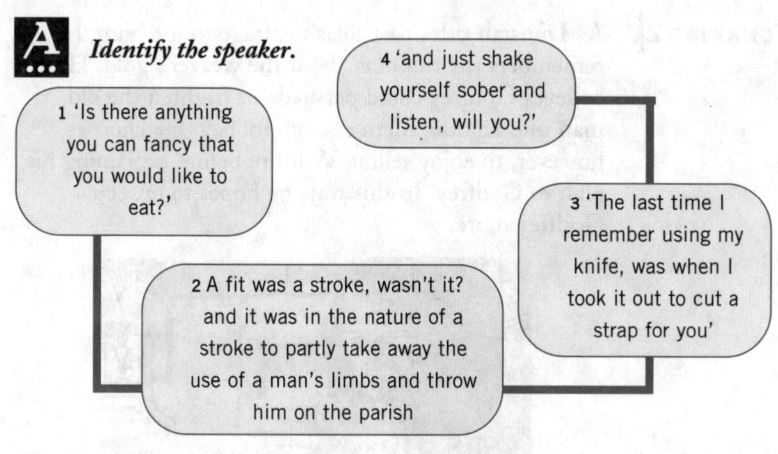

Identify the person 'to whom' this comment refers.

Check your answers on page 79.

B *Consider these issues.*

- **a** Why the author uses an old-fashioned opening (in which she refers to past events, objects, old styles of dress, language and using structures that were already dated in 1861) rather than an opening that is obviously openly trying to gain our interest.
- **b** The advantages and disadvantages of using a narrator to tell the story.
- **c** How the author makes us side with Silas.
- **d** How the author tells us about Silas's past.
- **e** What we learn about community and religion.
- **f** What the author makes us feel about the Cass family.
- **g** The effects of isolation and superstition on the residents of Raveloe.

A THEFT AND A DISAPPEARANCE, VILLAGE CONCERNS

CHAPTER 4

As Dunstan rides past Silas's cottage to the hunt, he remembers the rumours about the weaver's gold. He believes Godfrey could persuade or frighten the old man into lending them enough money. He chooses, however, to enjoy selling Wildfire before explaining his plan to Godfrey. In this way, he hopes to upset Godfrey more.

A bargain is quickly made with Bryce who agrees to pay when the horse is delivered to Batherley stables. Then Dunstan decides on a day's hunting. Through Dunstan's careless riding, the horse falls at a hedge. It is pierced with a stake and dies. No-one sees the accident, and the uninjured Dunstan has various reasons against hiring a horse in Batherley. He thinks again of Silas's gold. He decides he will force Godfrey to borrow it immediately. He is glad of the increasing mist and darkness which hide the shame and peculiarity of his having to walk.

All gentlemen normally travel on horseback, only poor people go on foot.

Holding a whip makes him feel better, even though it is engraved with Godfrey's name. He is able to use it to feel his way. While he walks, he wonders how the weaver can be persuaded and bullied to lend his money. The sight of Silas's cottage lights makes him decide to act immediately himself.

Look for places where the weather conditions reflect actions and atmosphere.

Dunstan is surprised to find the cottage empty and unlocked. The key is holding roasting pork in position near the fire. He wonders if Silas has fallen into the nearby quarry, the Stone-pit. He jumps to the conclusion that the weaver is perhaps dead. This idea makes Dunstan think no-one will realise the money is gone. He begins to hunt for it. Cottages having limited hiding places, he quickly finds the two leather bags holding the gold hidden beneath loose bricks near the loom. Suddenly frightened, Dunstan decides to hide in the darkness outside the cottage. There he can think about what to do with the bags.

COMMENT

The unpleasantness of Dunstan Cass is directly revealed to us through the events of the day when the hunt meets at Batherley. Dunstan's theft links Silas with Godfrey Cass, preparing us for their interweaving parallel plots.

Ironically (see Literary Terms), Dunstan thinks Silas may have fallen to his death in the quarry. The bad weather and decreasing visibility prepare us for the death of Dunstan (pathetic fallacy – see Literary Terms).

George Eliot uses traditional images of light and dark to symbolise good and evil. A good example of this is Dunstan slipping into the darkness.

GLOSSARY

to cover woods or undergrowth sheltering the fox
'blood' a thoroughbred horse
pocket pistol hip flask for brandy
too pale a colour silver, not gold coins
jacks mechanism to turn a roasting spit

CHAPTER 5

Dunstan just misses Silas returning to enjoy his roast pork and his gold. Needing string for the next day, Silas had happily left his isolated cottage unlocked instead of delaying his dinner. He is so short sighted that he notices nothing different in his cottage. Once warm again, he decides to enjoy looking at his gold as he eats his meal.

The discovery of the empty hole is a shock. He searches everywhere before again feeling the empty hole. Then he sinks into the seat of his loom.

What are Silas's reactions to his loss?

He considers the possibility of a thief. The pouring rain has destroyed any footsteps. Rather than believe cruel spirits are hurting him a second time, he decides the local poacher, Jem Rodney, must be the robber. He rushes off to the Rainbow pub where he expects to find men with the authority to help him. Mrs Osgood's dance has removed the most important villagers, but the rest make a larger than usual group in the pub kitchen.

COMMENT

As in his previous trouble at Lantern Yard, Silas instinctively turns to his loom and works.

Despite all his previous experience and his own antisocial behaviour since coming to Raveloe, Silas still has faith in humans because he rushes to the Rainbow for help.

Silas is as good as Dunsey is bad. His only concern is to regain his gold, not to hurt or punish anyone. On the other hand, Dunsey had enjoyed the idea of frightening the old man.

GLOSSARY

horn lantern the lantern was made of animal horn, not glass

CHAPTER 6

What is the role of Mr Snell here?

We meet Mr Snell, landlord of the Rainbow, his cousin Bob Lundy the butcher, Mr Dowlas the farrier, Mr Macey the tailor and parish clerk, Mr Tookey the tailor and deputy clerk, and Ben Winthrop the wheelwright. The villagers talk covers a slaughtered cow; the Lammeter family who have sold it; some unkind teasing and jokes about Mr Tookey; Mr Macey's well-known information on the Lammeters;

a Lammeter–Osgood wedding; the previous owners of the Lammeters' rented farm and its possible ghost. A lively but unfinished argument on ghosts and fair bets ends the chapter.

Comment

We are introduced to the working men of the village enjoying their pipes, beer and leisurely conversation. They are described as a group and detailed information is given on individuals. The descriptions bring the characters to life, reflecting their separate personalities and showing village attitudes.

George Eliot here uses dialect (see Literary Terms) and dialogue (see Literary Terms) to bring us closer to the villagers and give us insight into their lives.

As a woman, George Eliot could never have been present in a village inn – making this description of the scene the more remarkable.

We hear how the villagers treated previous outsiders (an important theme) which can be contrasted with their treatment of Silas.

George Eliot uses different forms of humour (see Language and Style) which relieve the tension of Silas's loss. The trivial incidents seriously reported, the villagers' enjoyment of the retelling of well-known stories and their arguments paint a comic scene of rural life.

Glossary

fustian strong cotton cloth for jackets

Durham a breed of cow

drenching forcing medicine down an animal's throat

Queen's heads coins from the reign of Queen Anne (d. 1714) still circulating

Old Harry the devil

Chapter 7

Each of the villagers thinks that Silas is a ghost until he begs for help. He seems mad when he accuses Jem Rodney of theft. Mr Snell makes him sit down to dry

Look at how George Eliot created a tense atmosphere here.

out. He orders him to tell his story. Convinced by Silas's distress, the men believe he has been robbed by the devil. Their proof of Jem's innocence makes Silas regret and apologise for his accusation. He remembers when he himself was falsely accused. Mr Dowlas suggests they inform the village constable, Mr Kench, who is ill. They decide they need to appoint a substitute constable and inspect the scene of the crime. After argument, Mr Snell, who is suggested as deputy constable, and Mr Dowlas go with Silas to Mr Kench.

COMMENT

Silas appears like the ghosts the villagers have been discussing, at once changing the atmosphere from comfortable distant events as they are shocked into reality.

This is a turning point – Silas has only wanted his gold, now he discovers the warmth of the village community as they listen to his story. In turn, because he is half crazed by his genuine distress, their attitude changes and they react with caring concern.

As soon as the villagers' evidence clears Jem Rodney, Silas remembers his own pain from false accusation.

GLOSSARY

mushed crushed

nolo episcopari (*Latin*) the formal false modesty of 'I do not wish to be a bishop' before accepting the post

CHAPTER 8

After Mrs Osgood's party, Godfrey Cass does not worry about the absence of Dunstan and Wildfire. He is too busy enjoying memories of Nancy and blaming himself for his secret marriage. Next day he focuses on Silas's loss. Suggestions about the possible identity of the thief are made and rejected before Mr Snell remembers a visiting pedlar. He connects this pedlar with the tinder box discovered near Silas's cottage. Other details about the robbery have to be discussed in the pub by the men. Silas gladly believes the pedlar was the thief but Godfrey does not agree.

Worried the missing Dunstan is spending his money, Godfrey rides off for news. He meets Bryce who tells him of the agreed sale and Wildfire's death. Believing the uninjured Dunstan will reappear to harm him, Godfrey eventually decides to tell his father everything on the next day.

He will tell him why he had lent the money, and of Wildfire's death. He will also reveal his secret marriage, because his wife has threatened to arrive at the Red House.

Look for other places where Godfrey hopes luck will help him.

He goes to bed having rehearsed how best to break the news. He fears his father's violent anger and his habit of refusing to change his decisions. Godfrey hopes his father's pride will prevent him disinheriting his son. However, in the morning, he wakes to his old fears of disgrace and losing Nancy. He decides to confess only about the money.

COMMENT

George Eliot amuses us with the villagers' detective skills and obliging memories.

Godfrey's weak willpower is emphasised by his rehearsal of what he will tell his father. He decides to rely on luck to extricate him – a key part of his character.

GLOSSARY

tinder box contained flint and steel to make a light before matches were invented

sizes the assizes – old name for trials of serious offences; held quarterly before a visiting judge

CHAPTER 9

At a late breakfast, Godfrey has a talk with his father. Squire Cass explains he is too poor to replace Wildfire, whom he understands is only injured. This misunderstanding makes Godfrey's confession about

Look at the Squire's attitude to his sons – what kind of father has he been?

Fowler's rent even harder. The Squire threatens to throw out all his sons and to remarry. He guesses the absent Dunstan has blackmailed Godfrey to lie over a guilty secret.

Ignoring his own bad land management and his past refusals of Godfrey's help, the Squire blames his increasing money problems on his sons. He offers to ask Nancy Lammeter to marry Godfrey. He believes Nancy could make Godfrey's decisions for him, and help him reform.

The Squire orders Godfrey to cancel the instructions against Fowler and orders instead the sale of Dunstan's horse. Pleased to have sorted the rent money, Godfrey worries that a possible chat between the Squire and Nancy's father might force him to have to refuse to marry her. Like most people with problems, Godfrey hopes luck will save him. The narrator warns us that most events are the results of actions we choose to do.

COMMENT

Further information is given on the character of Squire Cass. He hopes the war will continue, keeping prices high. He feeds meat to his dogs, in contrast to the villagers' diet (Dolly Winthrop treats Silas to lardy cakes in Chapter 10).

GLOSSARY

unstring open his purse

talking about peace the Napoleonic wars

collogue to plot

my property's got no entail on it an entail was a legal order of inheritance to a property – the Squire is free to disinherit all his sons

CHAPTER 10

Justice Malam orders a lengthy search for the pedlar which is unsuccessful. The Squire decides to refuse to have Dunstan home. Dunstan's continued absence upsets no-one. His disappearance is not linked to the robbery on the same day because of his respectable family and the mental effects on the villagers of the Christmas partying. Godfrey imagines him planning his troublemaking return.

The men of the village talk about the robbery in the Rainbow. Two rival opinions are strongly held by the villagers; either the pedlar, or evil spirits, have robbed Silas.

Silas moans softly at his work or by the fire at night. The villagers begin to pity him, deciding he is harmlessly crazy. They speak to him in the village and visit his cottage. Some give presents of food, in useless efforts to cheer him up. Several visitors give various reasons why Silas should be neighbourly and attend church.

We are introduced to Mrs Winthrop. The narrator tells us of her character and activities in the village before presenting us with her conversation with Silas. She makes Aaron, her seven-year-old son, sing a carol to Silas.

What can you find out about the villagers' attitudes to religion?

Despite the advice of his neighbours, Silas spends Christmas day alone, while the villagers go to church and feast. The Cass family, including their relatives Dr and Mrs Kimble, enjoy a family party. They do not mention or miss the absent Dunstan.

COMMENT

The villagers' changed attitude to Silas continues – they now regard him as crazy and needing help and sympathy. They encourage him to come to church – an important focus of community life – like the Rainbow.

Dolly's childlike religious faith and belief in Providence (God) is so simple as to be almost superstitious. For example, she puts the religious symbol IHS on her lardy cakes without understanding its meaning.

Dolly makes Aaron sing a carol as she believes it will do Silas good and encourage him to go to church. He is as bewildered by the music and 'church' as she is by the word 'chapel'.

The narrator looks forward to the greatest seasonal event, Squire Cass's annual New Year's Eve dance. This assembles everyone who is anyone, in either Raveloe or Tarley. It will last overnight, and contrasts starkly to Silas's lonely Christmas.

The author reminds us that Godfrey's problems remain unsolved. Dunstan's return and his father proposing for him are not Godfrey's only worries. He is still afraid he will be forced to refuse to marry Nancy because he is already married to Molly. Molly, meanwhile, is demanding money.

Godfrey's argument with himself, as the chapter ends, allows us into his mind. It shows us the conflict between what he ought to do and what he wants to do.

GLOSSARY

skimming dishes large shallow dishes used in dairy to allow cream to rise for skimming

yarbs herbs (in Midland accent)

the cussing of a Ash Wednesday reference to the Church Service on the first day of Lent

monthly nurse who looked after a new mother and baby for the first month

IHS Religious symbol for Latin abbreviation meaning Jesus

Athanasian Creed longer version of the Apostle's Creed which it replaces on festivals

TEST YOURSELF (Chapters 4–10)

A Identify the speaker.

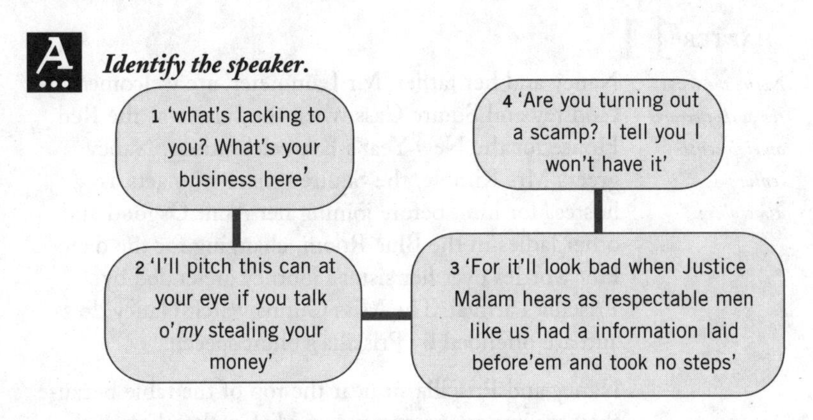

Identify the person 'to whom' this comment refers.

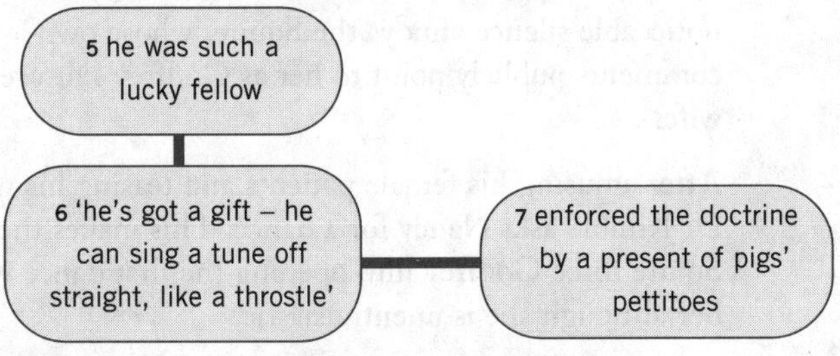

Check your answers on page 79.

B Consider these issues.

a The results of Dunstan Cass's actions on the day of the hunt.

b What we learn about the villagers individually, and their attitudes, as they enjoy their conversation in the Rainbow.

c How the author uses description and detail to make the period and Raveloe real to us.

d The reasons why Silas's appearance in the Rainbow is such a shock, and an evaluation of its importance.

e Any ways in which you notice the author balancing humour and suspense in this section.

f Your opinion of the role models given by Squire Cass as a father; a farmer; a landlord; and as the leader of Raveloe society.

NEW YEAR'S EVE AND EPPIE'S CHILDHOOD

CHAPTER 11

Notice the ways the author creates an eighteenth-century atmosphere.

Nancy and her father, Mr Lammeter, are welcomed by Godfrey and Squire Cass when they arrive at the Red House for the New Year's Eve celebrations. Nancy greets Mrs Kimble, the Squire's sister who acts as hostess for him, before joining her Aunt Osgood and other ladies in the Blue Room, changing for the dance. Her worries over her sister's journey are ended by Priscilla's arrival. The Miss Gunns watch Nancy dress and are offended by Priscilla's blunt speech.

Nancy and Priscilla sit near the top of the table because they are important guests and Mr Crackenthorpe, the Rector, compliments Nancy's looks. Godfrey's noticeable silence annoys the Squire, whose own comments publicly point to her as Godfrey's future wife.

After amusing his female patients and teasing his wife, Dr Kimble asks Nancy for a dance. This makes the Squire force Godfrey into opening the first dance with her although she is unenthusiastic.

As Solomon Macey leads the procession from the parlour to the White Parlour for dancing, Mr Macey, Ben Winthrop and other privileged villagers watch and pass comments. They guess Godfrey and Nancy are a couple. The real reason why these two leave the dance is because Nancy's damaged dress needs Priscilla's repairs. In the small parlour Nancy is deliberately cool to Godfrey until, carried away, he startles her into anger. This pleases him because it shows she still cares for him.

COMMENT

This chapter introduces Nancy Lammeter. Details and author's comments establish her appearance and character.

The lively description of the preparations for, and the

events of, the party give much detailed information on the period: of travel; of fashion; of contrasting ideas on fashion and social position in town and country; of a country festival.

Priscilla Lammeter is an engaging contrast to Nancy and to the Miss Gunns with their town ideas. She is a practical, hard-working, blunt-speaking countrywoman. She chooses to remain unmarried, unusual for women at that time.

The discussion in the Rainbow (Chapter 6) revealed the individual personalities and attitudes of the village men; this chapter does the same for the higher social group in the village. There is a sense of community as the watching villagers comment and generally approve.

George Eliot here draws attention to Nancy's country accent which would be used by all the villagers regardless of class. She mocks the town superiority of the Miss Gunns.

GLOSSARY

joseph a long cloak worn by women when riding

horseblock a stone block with steps, used to mount and dismount

bandboxes light boxes for holding headwear

shortest waists fashion of the period, waists of dresses high above natural body waists

skull cap and front a close-fitting cap with attached artificial hair which lay on the forehead

turban worn over the above article – very fashionable at the time

Dame Tedman's a village school run by untrained teacher

mawkin a scarecrow

tithe church tax from medieval times, originally one tenth of income paid in produce, not money

springe dialect word (see Literary Terms) meaning active

piert dialect word meaning lively, cheerful

CHAPTER 12

Look at George Eliot's use of language and figures of speech

While Godfrey talks to Nancy at the party, his wife, Molly Farren, carries her child towards Raveloe. She plans to tell the Squire she is Godfrey's secret wife. She intends to arrive at the party in her rags. This will hurt Godfrey more. She has not used his money to buy food and clothes. Instead, she has bought opium to which she is addicted. Darkness falls as she walks, exhausted, along the unfamiliar lanes. Craving her opium, she takes a dose before collapsing in the snow. She falls under a gorse bush.

As the unconscious Molly's arms lose their hold, her sleeping child wakes up. It toddles towards the light from Silas's open door. It reaches his fireplace where it falls asleep in the warmth.

Silas had begun looking out of his open door at nights. The villagers have told him to listen to the New Year bells which will bring him luck. Perhaps also his lost money will return. The door remains open while he has one of his fits. On recovering, he notices nothing changed inside his home.

As he bends to mend the fire, he thinks he sees his returned gold on the floor. His poor eyesight prevents his seeing the fair-haired sleeping child. Touching the child, he thinks he is dreaming of his own small sister. The child seems to have been sent by Providence. He comforts and feeds it when it awakes crying for its mother. Its uncomfortable wet boots remind Silas that the child is real. He finds the footprints which lead to Molly's body half buried by snow.

COMMENT

George Eliot makes use of coincidence (see Literary Terms) here: Molly collapses outside Silas's cottage, the door is open for the New Year's bells and Silas has a fit. The child is able to walk into his cottage.

This is one of the parallels George Eliot uses. Robbery led Silas to shut out people after Lantern Yard. Robbery in Raveloe causes him to accept their influence again. This highlights how Silas is changing.

Years before Silas had loved and cared for his small sister. Since leaving Lantern Yard he has cared for no-one. Receiving care in his own distress from the villagers, here he is able to comfort and care for the child who is in even greater need. His return to being able to love has started.

GLOSSARY

draughts of forgetfulness George Eliot uses this metaphor (see Literary Terms) – that Nancy acts on Godfrey like a pain-relieving drug – just as his wife, Molly, takes a real drug, opium, to ease the misery in her life

demon Opium an example of George Eliot using personification (see Literary Terms) to increase horror at the drug's effects. The drug becomes a living monster

CHAPTER 13

Squire Cass's party goes well and family, guests and servants watch Bob Cass dance; but Godfrey watches Nancy. Silas enters carrying the child whom Godfrey immediately recognises as his own. Silas asks Doctor

Kimble to attend the dying or dead woman in the snow.

Godfrey Cass hopes his wife is dead. He claims ignorance of his child as he answers the ladies' questions. Refusing Mrs Kimble's suggestion, Silas claims his right to keep the child. Godfrey controls his feelings as he leaves with Dr Kimble. He is praised by Dolly Winthrop as he brings her to Silas's cottage.

Notice the allusion which prepares us for the results of Godfrey's actions.

Godfrey guiltily decides not to identify Molly and his child as they would cost him Nancy. If Molly dies, he will be free to marry again. The child can be cared for and he will reform by marrying Nancy. Godfrey makes an excuse to see the dead woman. Sixteen years later he remembers every detail of his dead wife's face. He is pleased yet sorry that his daughter cannot recognise him. Silas decides to keep the child and Godfrey feels better after giving him money for her keep.

Only the absent Dunstan can harm Godfrey, who decides secrecy is best for himself, Nancy and his child.

COMMENT

The plots of Silas Marner and Godfrey Cass meet when Silas accepts the child and Godfrey rejects her.

George Eliot stresses that Godfrey recognises his duty as father to the child through references to his mental struggle. Because he is selfish and weak, he prefers to try to marry Nancy and chooses to disown the child.

Godfrey's actions to those he should love, his wife and child, are in sharp contrast to Dolly's. She puts herself out for a stranger in need; her husband and Mrs Snell can be relied on to help. This demonstrates the villagers' sense of community.

Dolly's praise of Godfrey is ironic (see Literary Terms) – his motive is to make sure Molly is dead; it is not tender hearted to disown his child. It is also ironical that sixteen years later he tries to regain his child.

GLOSSARY

the parish the workhouse, greatly feared by the poor, which was paid for by the parish rate

CHAPTER 14

Molly Farren's apparently unimportant death permanently affects several lives.

Raveloe quickens its changing attitude to Silas because he adopts the orphan. They are interested in how he will cope. The women are generous with advice and warnings. Silas confides in and receives practical help and advice from Dolly Winthrop. She approves of his keeping the child.

How does George Eliot create humour in describing Eppie's upbringing?

Silas continues to link his loss of money with the child's arrival. He is determined to have all her love. Dolly asks Silas to have the child christened and to bring her to church. Silas agrees, although he cannot connect Dolly's religion with his own past beliefs and experiences. She is surprised that Hephzibah (Eppie for short) is a bible name. Church attendance, together with Eppie's needs and interests, brings Silas into contact with the villagers. Silas discusses with Dolly how to punish Eppie but cannot bear to actually punish her. Together Silas and Eppie enjoy the countryside and Silas revives emotionally. The villagers and their children welcome Silas because of Eppie. His earnings become of little interest or value to him unless Eppie needs something. Silas accepts the villagers' advice. He is a changed man.

COMMENT

On the title-page of the first edition, George Eliot quoted William Wordsworth (a poet) about the effects following the arrival of a child. In this chapter Silas begins to change because of Eppie – this is an important theme.

The religion of the town chapel is very different from the established church. Silas does not understand

Dolly's religion. He agrees to have Eppie christened and brings her to church because he wants to do everything helpful to her and live by Raveloe customs. Now he is choosing to join the village community.

GLOSSARY

scratch just managing to make a living
moithered bewildered, bothered
ringing pigs to put rings in pigs' noses
'I believe' opening words of Apostle's Creed – a prayer
'noculation smallpox inoculation
colly dialect (see Literary Terms) – to blacken with coal dust
the gold which needed nothing Eppie's golden hair is an image (see Literary Terms) linked throughout the story with the lost gold. The effect of the gold was to shut Silas away, but Eppie's needs and demands force Silas to join the village. He becomes human again
brownie a helpful goblin
the city of destruction George Eliot refers to two possible allusions (see Literary Terms). In the Old Testament, angels led Lot and his wife away from Sodom before it was destroyed (Genesis 19). In *Pilgrim's Progress*, written in 1678 by John Bunyan, Christian is led away from the City of Destruction

CHAPTER 15

Look for places where Godfrey believes money will solve problems.

Godfrey Cass secretly watches Eppie grow and occasionally, as chance offers, gives small presents to Silas. No longer afraid of the absent Dunstan, he feels reformed and looks forward to marriage and a family with Nancy. Eppie will be provided for.

COMMENT

Godfrey is happy to have disowned Eppie.

This short chapter is packed with irony (see Literary Terms). Ironically, the weak and selfish Godfrey is not the reformed man he believes himself to be. His gifts to Silas depend on chance and he promises to himself to help Eppie – in the future. His marriage will be built on a lie. Ironic also is his dream of playing with his children – he will be childless. The chapter ends ironically – a father's duty does not end with providing money for a child. The previous chapter details the hours of devoted love Silas puts into bringing up Eppie. The contrast between Silas and Godfrey is again highlighted.

GLOSSARY

that famous ring in a fairy story, a ring pricked the prince who wore it whenever he prepared to do wrong

TEST YOURSELF (Chapters 11–15)

Identify the speaker.

1 'As I say, Mr Have-your-own-way is the best husband, and the only one I'd ever promise to obey'

2 'Ha, Miss Priscilla, the sight of you revives the taste of that super-excellent pork-pie'

3 'It does make her look funny, though – partly like a short-necked bottle wi'a long quill in it'

4 'I think those have the least feeling that act wrong to begin with'

Identify the person 'to whom' this comment refers.

5 (her) mind resembled her aunt's to a degree that everybody said was surprising, considering the kinship was on Mr ...'s side

6 His spare but healthy person, and high featured firm face, that looked as if it had never been flushed by excess

7 She needed comfort, and she knew but one comforter

Check your answers on page 79.

B ***Consider these issues.***

a What Mrs Osgood thinks of her nieces, Priscilla and Nancy Lammeter.

b What we learn about differences in lives and attitudes in town and country through the ladies in the Blue Room dressing for the party.

c What we discover about the characters and attitudes of the gentry of Raveloe from Squire Cass's party.

d What Godfrey Cass thinks of his wife Molly Farren and how he came to his opinion.

e The actions and attitudes of Silas and Godfrey to the small child.

f Light; dark; gold, the colour and the money; are just some of the images and symbols (see Literary Terms) George Eliot uses. Decide what they represent and whether you find them useful.

CHAPTER 16

Sixteen years have changed the villagers. Squire Cass is dead. Mr and Mrs Godfrey Cass are described leaving Sunday church followed by Mr Lammeter and Priscilla.

Collect details of cottage life reflecting happiness and social conditions.

Silas and Eppie discuss a garden which Aaron Winthrop promises to start that afternoon. At home they enjoy their dinner and Silas smokes his pipe outside while Eppie clears away.

Silas eventually has been able to discuss with Dolly the false accusation against him at Lantern Yard. They agree it was a test of his Christian faith, which he has regained through Eppie.

When Eppie joins Silas, she suggests a wall to protect the garden which will also include the gorse bush where her mother died. Demonstrating the stones nearby which are available for the wall, she notices the newly lowered water level in the quarry. Silas explains that it results from drainage ordered by Mr Cass to improve the land he has acquired from Mr Osgood.

Eppie speaks to Silas about her marrying Aaron. The young man has suggested they should then all live together. Silas decides to consult Dolly. He points out to Eppie that one day she will need the care of a younger man to replace himself.

COMMENT

George Eliot uses a timeshift to move the story forward sixteen years.

Detailed description shows the physical and mental changes between Silas and Eppie and the Winthrops. We see their happy home life, and learn of the changes a child has made to Silas – a major theme.

Village opinion approves of the gifts and cottage improvements made by Mr Cass. Silas is greatly admired by the villagers, who feel he deserves his good luck.

Eppie and Silas demonstrate their love by their tact and consideration for each other in discussing her marriage.

Silas confides about his past to Dolly whose faith explains it as a test from God. The reasons are unimportant to humans. Silas has enough faith to accept this idea.

George Eliot uses humour about the pipe to show how Silas accepts advice.

GLOSSARY

lavender traditionally planted by a man for his bride, it was used to scent linen and prevent moth attack

the weaving was going down the growth of factories resulted in the decline of the hand loom weaver

the gods of the hearth refers to household gods of ancient Rome

mine own famil'ar friend ... heel again me quotation from Psalm 41. Most people were familiar with the Bible; here Silas quotes it when trying to connect it with himself and his experience. The language he uses here in daily speech was similar to that of Bible translations used then

CHAPTER 17

Nancy's changes to the Red House are described as Priscilla and Mr Lammeter prepare to leave after Sunday dinner. Priscilla approves of Godfrey's farming changes. Maybe a dairy will cheer Nancy who is upset by Godfrey's unhappiness at being childless.

Look for Godfrey's thoughts about adopting Eppie.

Godfrey walks his land on Sunday afternoons while Nancy holds the Bible and thinks. Since their stillborn baby fourteen years before, she has twice refused Godfrey's wish to adopt Eppie. Nancy believes Providence intends them to be childless.

The servant arrives early with tea. She enjoys alarming

Nancy over the villagers' unusual activity. Nancy is afraid and wishes Godfrey would return.

COMMENT

George Eliot reflects a moral tone as Godfrey begins to reap what he has sown.

Nancy is a good woman who loves her husband. Her personality is limited, as forecast in Chapter 11, by the rigidity of her methods and her narrow view of Providence. Her argument against adopting Eppie is based on hearsay of one case.

Godfrey's unhappiness at being childless is increased by his secret knowledge that he alone is to blame. By disowning Eppie, he gave her to Silas. Unaware Godfrey is Eppie's father, Nancy's narrow religious views make her against adoption.

Nancy and Godfrey recognise good qualities in each other. Nancy feels she was right to refuse to adopt Eppie. Godfrey feels the truth about Eppie would kill Nancy's love for him even if it did not kill her. Their childless marriage seems his punishment for disowning Eppie.

As Eppie's birth father, Godfrey believes adopting her will be easy. He fails to understand the love between Silas and Eppie and the hurt he will cause. He lists to himself the social advantages of adoption to Eppie. Because he does not know Silas, Godfrey thinks he will agree.

GLOSSARY

Derbyshire spar crystal naturally occurring in parts of England, here probably of Derbyshire 'Blue John'

the increasing poor rate and the ruinous times the Napoleonic wars had kept the price of corn artificially high and the drop in price, following peace, hit farmers like Mr Lammeter and Godfrey hard. Increased unemployment, of the returning soldiers, resulted in higher taxes on the parish rate, to pay for higher costs from the increased numbers on relief money given to the poor at home or in the work house

Michaelmas feast of St Michael (29 September), one of the four Quarter days when rural wages and bills were paid and people changed employment

something to fill your mind irony (see Literary Terms) since Nancy and Godfrey will not only think of their new milk herd and dairy – the land drainage reveals Dunstan's skeleton and will result in plenty to think over.

Mant's Bible one of the few objects which help fix the period. First published in 1816 and named from the commentary written by Richard Mant, Bishop of Down

transported many criminals were despatched to Australia, often for trivial offences

raven traditionally referred to in literature as an omen of disaster

CHAPTER 18

Godfrey enters in shock, ending Nancy's relief at his return. He tells her of the discovery and identification of Dunstan's skeleton in the newly drained Stone-pit.

Has Godfrey really changed?

She is surprised at the strength of his reaction, until he tells her that Dunstan stole Silas's gold. It lies in the quarry beside the skeleton. Disgraced by Dunstan's theft, and at last determined to hide nothing, Godfrey tells Nancy the truth about his first wife. She learns that Eppie is his child.

Godfrey's excuse is that the truth would have lost him Nancy. Nancy feels she would have accepted Eppie as Godfrey's daughter. Their married life might have been very different. She tells Godfrey that Eppie has been wronged and nothing is worth committing injustice.

Again Godfrey realises he is defeated by his own faults. He decides to approach Eppie that night, although Nancy warns him of difficulties.

COMMENT

Nancy's rigid beliefs benefit Godfrey – she does not leave him to return to her father as he fears. She sticks by him and agrees he must do his duty by Eppie.

In the previous chapter, Godfrey misjudged Silas, here he misjudges his wife who surprises him with her generous reaction.

Godfrey is unable to empathise with Silas and Eppie and how they will feel. Nancy has greater insight – she expects difficulties because of Eppie's age.

TEST YOURSELF (Chapters 16–18)

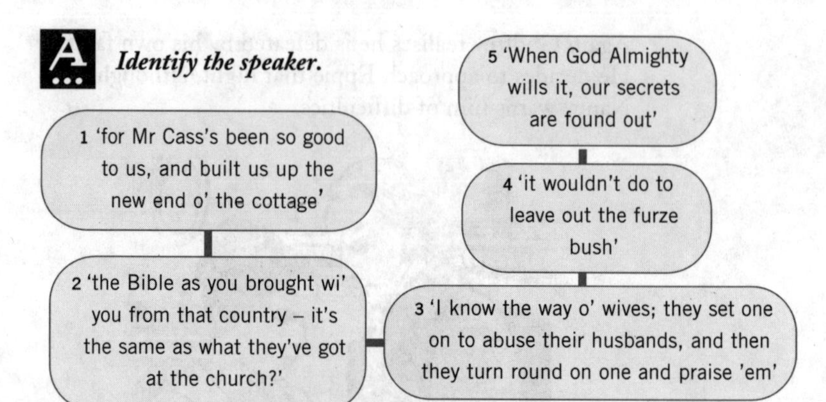

A *Identify the speaker.*

Identify the person 'to whom' this comment refers.

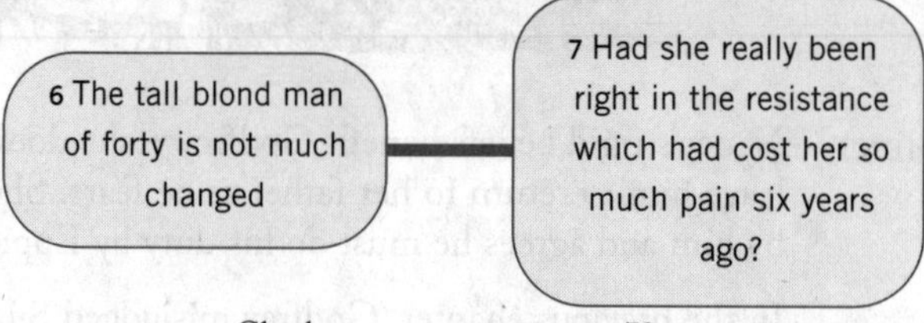

Check your answers on page 79.

Consider these issues.

- **a** How Silas and Eppie feel about Godfrey Cass.
- **b** The importance of Dolly's religion.
- **c** The significance of Eppie's garden and the draining of the Stone-pit.
- **d** The advantages and disadvantages of how the author reveals the lives of Silas and Godfrey to us.
- **e** How and why the author makes us interested in her female characters and which she prefers.
- **f** Nancy's views on adoption and the results of Silas adopting Eppie.

CHAPTER 19

Later that night, Silas speaks of his misery and his need for the gold before Eppie's arrival. They speak of their love for each other. Silas explains that the returned gold is useful but he is free from its spell.

Mr and Mrs Cass arrive and Godfrey apologises for Dunstan's theft of Silas's gold. Eppie's garden provides Godfrey's excuse to talk about her future. Silas feels hurt and uneasy listening to Godfrey's plans. He invites Eppie to reply for herself. She refuses Godfrey's offer of adoption; she cannot leave the people she knows and loves. She is content and does not wish to be a lady. Upset by the refusal of his plans, Godfrey's anger leads him to reveal Eppie's parentage. He cannot understand Silas's point of view.

Compare and contrast Godfrey and Silas as fathers.

As Godfrey and Silas argue, Godfrey masks his selfishness by talking about Eppie's gain. Silas replies truthfully from his heart although he is afraid of blocking her opportunities. Silas again invites Eppie to choose her future life, this time knowing her birth father. Nancy sympathises with Silas's position but, because of her social class and love for Godfrey, she believes her husband to be in the right.

Silas withdraws his objections and does not try to influence Eppie's choice. This makes Nancy and Godfrey think that she will agree to their offer. However, Eppie carefully explains her reasons for refusing. Nancy suggests Eppie should agree to Godfrey's wishes because he is her legal father. Eppie only recognises one father: Silas. She explains that she plans to continue living with him. She will care for him with the help of the man she has promised to marry. Godfrey had felt very noble about his decision to adopt Eppie. He considers his rejection of her as a baby to be the worst action of his life. Eppie's refusal means he is prevented from feeling good about her. Very upset, he quickly leaves the cottage. Nancy follows him after promising to visit again.

COMMENT

As the chapter opens, George Eliot creates a rather grim humour through irony (see Literary Terms).

Silas is counting his blessings as Godfrey and Nancy arrive to claim Eppie. He is threatened with losing her (his new treasure – p. 137) on the day his old treasure returns.

What makes a lady?

Nancy feels they are disturbing Silas and Eppie 'very late' – sixteen years late! Godfrey should have claimed Eppie as a baby. Godfrey will 'make a lady' of Eppie. Silas always feels uneasy when his 'betters' like Mr Cass are present.

Again the paths of Silas and Godfrey meet through Eppie – the two plots converge.

Duty is insisted on by Godfrey (because it now, selfishly, pleases him) and Nancy tells Eppie that in law she owes it to Godfrey (something unpleasant she must do). Contrast their ideas of duty with Eppie's feelings about the people she has grown up with and loves.

GLOSSARY

'beauty born of murmuring sound' a quotation from one of the *Lucy* group of poems by William Wordsworth (1770–1850)

CHAPTER 20

We follow Nancy's and Godfrey's return home. They realise Eppie will never be their daughter. In the circumstances they agree to continue hiding that Godfrey is Eppie's birth father. He decides to reveal it in his will. He has had enough of hidden crimes like Dunstan's. Nancy is relieved that her relations will only know of Dunstan's robbing Silas.

What is your opinion on Godfrey and his position?

Godfrey guesses that Eppie will marry Aaron Winthrop. Nancy feels Aaron is a good choice because he is serious and hard working. They discuss Eppie's character and her resemblance to Godfrey. He feels that his punishment for rejecting her is that she dislikes and will misjudge him. Nancy feels it is right that Godfrey suffers. She tries to cheer him up by telling him he has always been a good husband. She encourages him to try to accept what has happened and the position he is in.

COMMENT

Godfrey's character has at last grown as he realises that some wrongs cannot be put right and that money cannot solve everything.

He comments on the irony (see Literary Terms) of his situation – he once wanted to appear to have no children, now he is forced to seem childless.

CHAPTER 21

The next day Silas tells Eppie that for some time he has wanted to revisit Lantern Yard. The return of his stolen gold makes such a visit possible. He wants to question the minister, Mr Paston, about the church money stolen so long ago. He also wants to tell him about religion as it is lived in Raveloe. For different reasons, both Eppie and Dolly think the visit a good idea.

Look for ways the author creates atmosphere and uses images.

At first Silas recognises nothing of the town where he grew up. Industry has changed it enormously in thirty years. He becomes excited when he recognises the town jail and the streets near Lantern Yard. Eppie is increasingly uneasy and upset by the town's size, activities and ugliness.

They discover that for more than ten years a large factory has stood on the site of Lantern Yard. This so shocks and upsets Silas that Eppie is afraid he will have a fit. No-one is able to tell Silas what happened to the chapel, its minister and congregation.

EPPIE'S CHOICE AND A WEDDING

Raveloe is now home to Silas. Dolly Winthrop comforts him when he tells her that the truth about the theft is lost forever. She points out that it remains true that Silas was wrongly accused. Maybe the supernatural powers wanted this to happen to him. It does not matter if she and he never understand the reasons for this. Silas agrees. Through Eppie, who has chosen to stay with him, he has recovered enough faith for the rest of his life.

COMMENT

The rapid changes of the Industrial Revolution have completely transformed the town. Silas and Eppie are both appalled by the conditions and noise. Prison Street and the jail are images of the misery of factory workers' lives.

Light and dark are images of faith. The town is dark and the streets narrow. The narrow religion of Lantern Yard has disappeared – the light Silas once lived by. Dolly told Silas she would be glad of any light he could bring back from his visit and comfortingly accepts the truth is in the dark unknown when he returns. Silas realises he himself received light (faith) when Eppie came. It will be enough, now she has promised to stay with him.

GLOSSARY

tassels on his shoulders the uniform of a commissionaire

CONCLUSION

Eppie and Aaron marry on a warm sunny day in early summer. Mrs Cass has given her the wedding dress of her dreams. She walks home from church between Aaron and Silas. Dolly and Ben Winthrop follow them. Arriving with her father for a day with Nancy, Priscilla enjoys watching the wedding group. It is a shame that Godfrey has had to go for the day to Litherley. He will miss his present of a reception at the Rainbow. It is right that he has helped Silas whom Dunstan had hurt. Priscilla feels Nancy would have been lucky to adopt a child like Eppie. She and her father agree they could enjoy a youngster.

Too disabled and old to go to the church or the reception, Mr Macey sits ready to give a speech to the passing wedding group. He reminds everyone that he was the first to stand up for Silas. He hopes the young couple will have good luck even though he could not take part in the service, and they have had to have Tookey instead.

Outside the Rainbow the villagers enjoy the time between the wedding and the meal. They respect Silas and agree he deserves good luck because of his treatment of Eppie. Ben Winthrop chooses to join his friends at the pub.

Contrast these images and atmosphere in this chapter to those in Chapter 21.

The other four go for a short interval back to Silas's cottage. His good landlord, Godfrey Cass, has extended and altered the cottage, and its large garden is complete. Eppie decides no-one could be happier or have a prettier home.

Comment

Notice the weather again fits human feelings – early summer sun shines on Eppie, in the wedding dress of her dreams, marrying the man she loves.

EPPIE'S CHOICE AND A WEDDING

Priscilla's and Mr Lammeter's discussion revives the theme of a child's influence transforming lives. It is ironic (see Literary Trems) that if Godfrey had been a true father, Nancy would have brought up the child.

Mr Macey is triumphant to be right that Silas was harmless and his gold did return. The village opinion is that Silas deserves his good luck by acting as a father to the orphan.

Godfrey has generously provided the wedding feast but has absented himself for the day. It is Silas who appears as Eppie's father. The villagers feel Godfrey's action is right, considering the hurt Dunsey did to Silas. Ironically, Godfrey's secret wrong to Eppie was greater.

George Eliot ends the book with conventional happiness which reflects the moral code approved at the time of writing – the good are rewarded while the evil are punished.

TEST YOURSELF (Chapter 19–Conclusion)

A Identify the speaker.

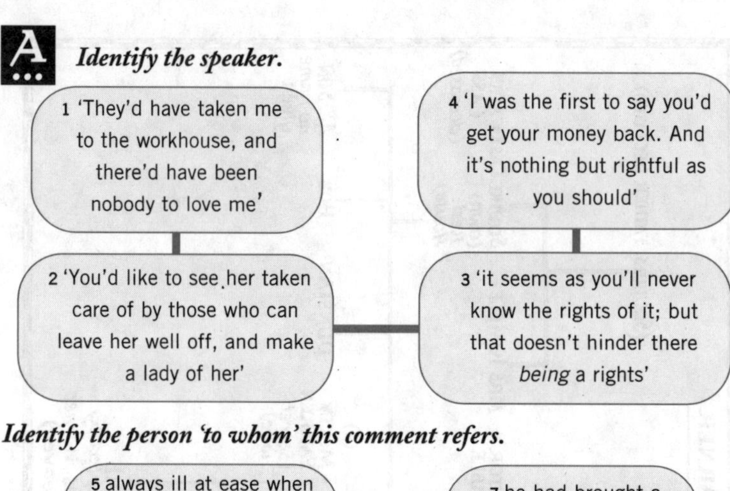

Identify the person 'to whom' this comment refers.

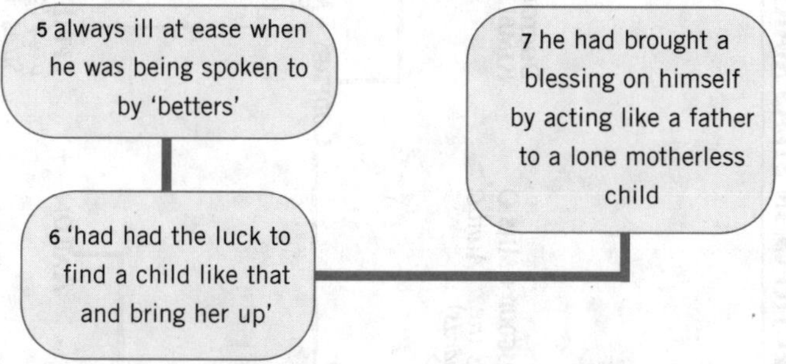

Check your answers on page 79.

B Consider these issues.

a Make your own list of qualities needed by a father and compare and contrast Silas and Godfrey.

b Why the reader's knowledge of the decision to adopt is important when Silas talks about his gold and Eppie.

c Whether Nancy or Eppie is more of a 'lady'.

d The viewpoints of the participants discussing Eppie's future and the Cass' unsuccessful adoption offer.

e How the author makes readers aware of rapid changes in society and living conditions.

f Silas's personality and position in the village when Eppie marries.

g How you feel about the ending of the novel.

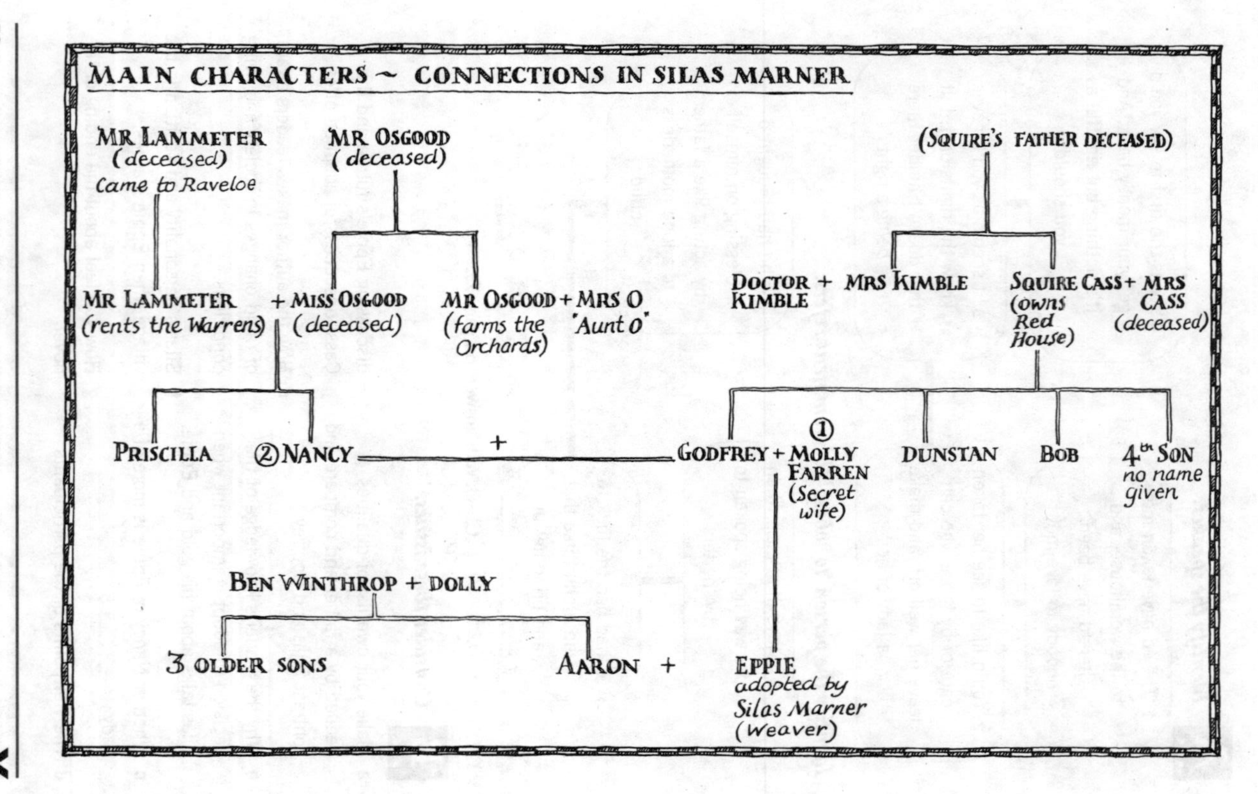
MAIN CHARACTERS ~ CONNECTIONS IN SILAS MARNER
MR LAMMETER (deceased)
Came to Raveloe
MR OSGOOD (deceased)
(SQUIRE'S FATHER DECEASED)
MR LAMMETER (rents the Warrens)
+ MISS OSGOOD (deceased)
MR OSGOOD + MRS O
(farms the Orchards)
"Aunt O"
DOCTOR KIMBLE + MRS KIMBLE
SQUIRE CASS (owns Red House) + MRS CASS (deceased)
PRISCILLA
② NANCY
+
GODFREY + ① MOLLY FARREN (Secret wife)
DUNSTAN
BOB
4th SON no name given
BEN WINTHROP + DOLLY
3 OLDER SONS
AARON
+
EPPIE adopted by Silas Marner (Weaver)

COMMENTARY

THEMES

Five main themes are discussed here – there are other issues and concerns which you can enjoy finding for yourself as you study the text.

EVERYDAY LIFE

During the book's thirty-year time span (1790–1820), George Eliot shows the great changes in daily life brought by the Industrial Revolution. Much of England's population shifted from rural agricultural to urban industrial society. By the end of the novel, she contrasts town conditions and attitudes (Chapter 21) to those of the country which are given throughout the book.

She recreates the period and its atmosphere through information and details on daily life provided by:

- Raveloe village and its area (Chapters 1, 2)
- Outsiders – newcomers or people different in any way (Chapters 1, 2)
- Housing (Chapters 1, 3, 4, 11, 12)
- The gentry (Chapters 3, 11)
- Festivals and celebrations (Chapters 11, 13)
- Attitudes – between the villagers and the gentry (Chapters 3, 9, 11, 13)
- The villagers (male) – work, interests and leisure (Chapter 6)
- Parenting (Chapters 3, 10, 14, 15, 19)
- Religion (Chapters 1, 10, 14)
- Superstition (Chapters 1, 6)
- Education and childcare (Chapter 14)
- Health and community care (Chapters 1, 11, 13).
- Clothes and fashion (Chapters 6, 11, 22)

- Country activities, conditions, attitudes (throughout)
- Town conditions and attitudes (Chapters 1, 11, 21)

RELIGION

Young people, brought up by a deeply religious person or in a strongly religious environment, like the young Silas Marner and the young George Eliot, may not challenge their beliefs.

Think about the purpose of religious practices and discussions in Silas Marner.

The life and work of John Wesley (1703–91) had great appeal to poorly educated working people, especially those in towns. Small sects like the chapel congregation of Lantern Yard grew up in imitation of his followers who became known as Methodists because of their hardworking simple lives and orderly worship based on the Bible. They were also called evangelicals (after the New Testament writers) and non-conformists because they did not accept the established Church of England. They also rejected its organisational structure; believing that all Christians are equal and replacing priests by ministers.

In contrast, the established church continued in its traditional way, especially in country areas.

When thinking about the importance of religion in the novel, consider the following and find information on:

1) The chapel in Lantern Yard (Chapters 1, 2, 10, 14, 21)

2) The church in Raveloe (Chapters 2, 6, 10, 14, 16, 22)

For both the above, discover/think about:
- The beliefs held
- Its organisation; how it was run
- Its membership
- Attitudes to it
- Attitudes it encouraged

Consider the practical effects on peoples' lives from both chapel and church:
- On their beliefs

- On their attitudes to others
- On their actions
- On their lives

Perhaps George Eliot intended you to reach conclusions about how religion affected people both in the town and in the country.

DUTY

Duty was very important to the Victorian readers for whom George Eliot wrote. Those characters in the book who fail in their duty must be punished and those who do their duty must be rewarded. It is closely connected to a sense of justice and moral awareness. It involves our responsibilities to others and can come from our circumstances, from our beliefs, or both.

Compare and contrast this idea of duty with its treatment in a modern world.

In *Silas Marner* duty is presented through parenting and community. We have many examples of parents – natural and adoptive – if they do their duty their children turn out well; if neglected they turn out badly (except Eppie whom Silas adopts). Consider the parenting by the following, and the resulting children:

Parents	*Child*
Squire Cass (pp. 24, 68) – punished	Godfrey (p. 24) – weak, selfish
	Dunstan (p. 24) – vicious, evil
Godfrey (p. 172) – punished	Eppie (p. 118) – consier the result if she had gone, as would have been expected, to the workhouse
Dolly Winthrop and Ben (p. 48)	Aaron (p. 181)
Mr Lammeter (pp. 25, 98) – rewarded	Priscilla (p. 152) – cares for her aged father
Silas (pp. 118, 129) – adopts Eppie, rears and cares for her	Eppie (pp. 173, 183) – rewards Silas's parents

In the same way the characters receive justice – the good (Silas) are rewarded and the evil (Dunstan and Godfrey) are punished.

COMMUNITY

A sense of community is an important theme in the novel – it links very closely with themes on people and environment, outsiders and no man is an island – all human actions bring results – open or secret. Because the community at Lantern Yard wrongly accuse Silas of theft and expel him (p. 13), Silas comes to Raveloe (p. 7). He visits neither the church nor the pub (p. 8) where the community meet, and he refuses through his unfriendly behaviour (p. 19) to become part of the village. In turn, the villagers' primitive sense of community makes them suspect and fear newcomers like Silas (p. 19), especially when he is so different from them in so many ways.

A second theft (p. 40), the loss of his gold, makes Silas seek the help of the community (p. 44) and the villagers support him (p. 59).

By adopting Eppie (p. 118) Silas saves the community her cost to the poor rate. This pleases and interests the community (p. 129). Eppie leads Silas into church and community (p. 130) – he is accepted and approved long before his adopted daughter marries into the community (p. 181).

THE EFFECT BROUGHT BY A CHILD

This is another major theme and connects with parenting, duty and community. A child has a ripple effect on the lives of the surrounding people. This is recognised by Priscilla and Mr Lammeter (p. 182) as they watch the returning wedding group. Looking at Eppie, they both feel their age and miss the interest in life and the hopes brought by children and young people.

At the beginning of the novel Silas seems older than his actual age of around forty years (p. 20). His lonely, miserly life brings him no happiness (p. 16). He works 'like the spider' (p. 16) without 'love and fellowship' (p. 17). Like all weavers, his figure 'shrank and bent' (p. 20) through the weaving and the weight of his 'heavy bag' (p. 5).

As a result of Eppie's arrival, he is able to carry a much heavier load – Eppie and 'his yarn or linen at the same time' (p. 129) and he goes 'strolling out' (p. 126) with all the time in the world to enjoy nature and the countryside.

STRUCTURE

Silas Marner has been written in two parts a larger Part One and a smaller Part Two.

The narrative covers two periods of time in Part One:

- c.1805 – opening fifteen years after Silas arrived in Raveloe which records events from mid November into the New Year.
- c.1790 – a flashback to show Silas's experiences in Lantern Yard.

A third period of time is covered in Part Two:

- c.1821 – a timeshift to go forward to events sixteen years after the opening.

The plot of a book looks at patterns and connections between characters and events. As the book's plot presents the events of Silas's life, it also reveals:

- His early character and attitudes to him
- The causes of events which affect or change him
- His final character and attitudes to him

Throughout the book, George Eliot balances the plot structure through people and events. Look for the balance from:

- Mysterious appearances and mysterious disappearances
- Thefts and false accusations
- Examples of men/fathers and examples of women/mothers
- Types of religion and types of communities
- Examples of family life
- Town and country

In spite of the subtitle *The Weaver of Raveloe*, there is a second plot – the life of Godfrey Cass – which runs parallel to the story of Silas.

CHARACTERS

SILAS

Silas Marner, the skilled hand loom linen-weaver, of 'exemplary life and ardent faith' (p. 9), is the hero of George Eliot's novel. His trusting personality is basically good and attractive (p. 9) although his circumstances temporarily change him into an antisocial miser (p. 14). His simple religious faith was lived out through his hardworking and self-denying life. Both were much admired (p. 9) by the narrow-minded evangelical sect to which he belonged and generously contributed most of his earnings (p. 17). Even his cataleptic fits made him 'evidently a brother selected for a peculiar discipline' (p. 10).

Naïve
Vulnerable
Temporarily an 'Outsider'
Hardworking
Honest
Essentially loving

His naïve faith is so strong and sincere that his betrayal, by his friend William Dane and by God failing to clear him, results in his total loss of faith in people and God. His personality dramatically changes (p. 14).

He moves to a rural community whose suspicions and fears he increases by inviting 'no comer to step across his door-sill' (p. 7). He also never 'drinks a pint at the

Rainbow' nor enjoys 'gossip at the wheelwright's' (p. 8). He replaces friends by his obsession for his gold, for which he compulsively weaves. He remains in this numbed mechanical phase until circumstances again cause him to change. The theft of his gold makes him so desperate that he turns to the villagers for their help. They generously respond and feel he is more crazy than dangerous. Their advice and visits recognise his need.

'It's come to me' (p. 115), the mysterious arrival of the child seems almost supernatural to Silas. Impulsively he decides 'I've a right to keep it' and eventually, through the child, his life transforms a second time. In fact, his goodness, and other good qualities, had gone dormant and are reawakened through Eppie.

Through Eppie, he gains the friendship of Dolly Winthrop. In Dolly's wisdom and religious faith he finds peace over the false accusation of long ago, and regains his own faith in God (p. 180). Through what he does for Eppie and the change she brings to his personality, he becomes an admired and respected member of the village community (p. 182). He has earned his good luck, his enlarged and improved cottage, his returned gold and his happiness in living with and being cared for by his beloved daughter and her husband (p. 183).

EPPIE

Loving
Caring
Lively
Sensitive
Loyal
Joyful

Eppie is an idealised character. She is a pretty two-year-old with golden hair and blue eyes contrasting with her dirty, shabby clothes when she toddles into Silas's cottage. Aged three, she has a 'fine capacity for mischief' (p. 126) and loves the world and Silas (p. 130). She is important to both the plot and Silas's character – she is the means by which Silas recovers emotionally and becomes part of the village community. Her character though remains relatively flat (see Style) and undeveloped.

Sixteen years later, as an attractive and neat 'blond dimpled girl of eighteen' with 'curly auburn hair' (p. 138), she has a lively personality and is loving, generous and considerate of others. She is a good housekeeper in the happy home where she devotedly cares for her ageing father (p. 149). She sensitively wishes to marry using her dead mother's ring (p. 148). She is grateful to Silas for saving her from the workhouse and for his love and care (p. 166).

She has shy good manners to Nancy and Godfrey (p. 166), but shortly afterwards (p. 169) her shyness has gone when she declines their offer because of her love for Silas and the villagers. She is unmaterialistic and without social ambition (p. 169). Her shocked reaction on learning Godfrey is her father turns to repulsion (p. 171). She speaks with cold decision (p. 172) when she chooses Silas and remains faithful to her upbringing and friends (p. 173). Although excited and wanting to score off Aaron by visiting the town (p. 177), its reality shocks and horrifies her, and she cannot wait to be home (p. 178).

GODFREY

Godfrey Cass is ironically (see Literary Terms) described as 'fine, open-faced, good natured' by the approving villagers (p. 24) when he already has much to hide. He goes through life acting on impulses and hoping luck will save him from the results of his actions. In this way he has secretly married Molly Farren and fathered a child, been blackmailed to embezzle money due to his father – and yet still somehow hopes to wriggle out of everything and marry Nancy Lammeter! We are told he has an easy disposition and prefers good. For a while fortune favours him: Molly dies, Silas takes Eppie and Nancy agrees to marry him. With all his privileges and his loving wife, in the end Godfrey is unhappy because, ironically, he has to appear childless, his only child

Kindly
Weak
Selfish
Deceitful
Insensitive
Opportunist

apparently having died. He had a child whom he disowned – he did not deserve to be a father. Silas adopted the child and was truly a father to her.

Godfrey often seems to expect that money will solve his problems; he gives Molly money which she spends on opium; he gives Silas money when he adopts Eppie; he expects Silas and Eppie to agree to his adoption plans because of money, and finally, he pays for the wedding reception at the Rainbow.

The discovery of Dunstan's remains is a turning point in Godfrey's character when he admits 'When God Almighty wills it our secrets are found out' (p. 162). He tells Nancy every fact that he had hidden from her, about Molly being his wife and Eppie his daughter, only to realise 'he had not measured this wife with whom he had lived so long' (p. 163). Her surprising reaction makes him realise 'his error was not simply futile, but had defeated its own end' (p. 163). His brief satisfaction when Nancy agrees to adopt Eppie turns to punishment when Eppie says 'can't feel as I've got any father but one' (p. 173) and 'I should have no delight i' life any more if I was forced to go away from my father' (p. 172) i.e. Silas. At last Godfrey admits 'There's debts we can't pay like money debts … Marner was in the right' (p. 174). He recognises the irony of wanting 'to pass for childless once, Nancy – I shall pass for childless now against my wish' (p. 174).

DUNSTAN

Selfish
No morals
Vicious
Evil Bitter
Spiteful

Dunstan (nicknamed Dunsey) is all bad. He drinks, gambles and enjoys making other people unhappy. The villagers have a low opinion of him: 'a spiteful jeering fellow' (p. 24). He lies 'independent of utility' (p. 35). There is a suggestion that he tempted Godfrey into marrying Molly as 'the means of gratifying at once his jealous hate and his cupidity' (p. 31). Perhaps he is jealous of Godfrey: 'You're my elders and betters, you

know; I was obliged to come when you sent for me' (p. 25). He borrows and spends money recklessly. He blackmails his brother into 'borrowing' money from their father. He is overconfident – he believes he is lucky because 'whenever I fall, I'm warranted to land on my legs' (p. 30). He treats animals badly, killing Godfrey's horse Wildfire through his careless riding (p. 35). He has a sadistic streak – he enjoys the idea of forcing Silas to lend his money (p. 34). Walking home, he seizes the chance to steal the money hidden inside the empty cottage (p. 38). When he disappears, people feel 'It was no matter what became of Dunsey' (p. 24). It is the discovery of his body that forces Godfrey into telling Nancy the secrets of his past.

DOLLY

Motherly
Practical
Competent
Uncomplicated
Strong Christian faith
Non-judgmental

Dolly is a 'comfortable' woman, 'good-looking, fresh-complexioned', with 'lips always slightly screwed' and 'grave' expression (p. 80). Her physical looks are unimportant, in contrast to Nancy with her care of external appearances.

Like Nancy, she is widely admired as a good woman and excellent housewife, but Dolly 'was the person always first thought of in Raveloe when there was an illness or death' (p. 80). Unable to read, but practical and competent, she contentedly and sincerely lives 'her simple Raveloe theology' (p. 84).

Very poor, she prefers 'a bit o' bread' (p. 81) to the lardy cakes which she gives to Silas. The cakes, and later the baby clothes 'patched and darned, but clean and neat' (p. 121), are examples of her sensitive generosity.

Dolly's continued support 'without any show of bustling instruction' (p. 120) and 'with a woman's tender tact' (p. 122) turns her into Silas's valued friend as she enables him to rear her goddaughter, Eppie. Through her insistence that Silas 'take (Eppie) to church, and let her learn her catechise' (p. 123), Silas regains his religious faith as he becomes accepted, then admired by the villagers (p. 182).

NANCY

Morally good
Excellent housekeeper
Model wife
Mentally strict and narrow
Becomes humbler and forgiving

The character of Nancy develops through the complimentary details of her looks and reflects her shallow concern over appearances. Admired by everyone, she is 'beautiful', 'thoroughly bewitching' (p. 89), 'small and light' (p. 90), and 'dainty and neat' (p. 92). She is an outstanding and hardworking housewife (p. 92).

She loves her family and although minimally educated, with a broad local accent, she has 'the essential attributes of a lady' (p. 93).

Most importantly for the plot, Nancy is 'slightly proud and exacting' (p. 93) and rarely changes her mind. Her strict moral standards make her decide to refuse Godfrey (whom she loves) unless he reforms (p. 96).

Later, Nancy's looks and appearance reveal some personality growth. Her 'beauty has a heightened interest' (p. 137) and her 'firm yet placid mouth, the clear veracious glance' result from 'a nature that has been tested and kept its highest qualities' (p. 137). Her clothes still have 'dainty neatness and purity' (p. 137) and in her home 'all is polish' (p. 151).

She loves Godfrey and understands her 'best of husbands' (p. 153).

Her unchanged moral code makes her narrow and limited when she believes their baby's death and childlessness are 'Heaven's sending' (p. 156), making her selfishly refuse Godfrey's pleas to try and adopt Eppie (p. 156).

Her pride makes her feel characteristic shame (p. 162) over Dunstan's crime but we admire her surprising lack of anger (p. 163) and generous support when Godfrey confesses (p. 164).

She is humble enough to believe she was not 'worth doing wrong for' (p. 163).

MINOR CHARACTERS

IN TOWN

At Lantern Yard

William Dane is needed as a contrast to Silas and an example of the arrogant, confident person who could result from the narrow, exclusive group to which he belonged. He is able to betray Silas because he is as wicked as Silas is honest and trusting.

Sarah, Silas's betrothed, does not love him because her shallow affection allows her to follow public opinion against him and 'in little more than a month' (p. 14) to marry William.

At Batherley

Molly Farren, a former barmaid, first wife of Godfrey Cass and Eppie's mother, creates suspense before she dies in the snow through her plan to expose her husband to his proud father. Addicted to opium, love for her child prevents her quietening its hungry cries with the drug which she bought with Godfrey's money instead of food and clothes. She represents the life some women endured in the towns of the period, for which she blames Godfrey rather than herself.

IN THE COUNTRY

Raveloe villagers

The vividly described and highly individual villagers provide us with humour and reveal the village hierarchy and tensions.

Mr Snell is the landlord of the Rainbow public house, the classless heart of social life for the men of the village. He was always very careful never to take sides (p. 46), even when pushed by Mr Dowlas, the argumentative farrier (p. 47). He acts as prompter to old Mr Macey (p. 57) to take him through his repertoire of well-known stories. He is practical and comforting to the distraught Silas (p. 55), tells the angry Jem to be quiet (p. 56) and calmly refutes Silas's accusation of Jem (p. 57). A leader of the villagers, he is keen to be deputy constable and amuses us when he most obligingly 'gradually recovered a vivid impression' (p. 61) of the pedlar!

These highly individual villagers are great fun – enjoy them!

Bob Lundy the butcher, Mr Snell's cousin, is attractively presented as jolly, smiling and red haired. Also mild and 'I'm for peace' (p. 41), he is a slow countryman. He needs time to think about answers and has music in his soul.

Mr Dowlas, the opinionated and impulsive farrier, just has to be right – always! He is aggressive, able to become angry over nothing and uses 'bitter sarcasm' (p. 53). He is the 'negative spirit' and proud of it.

Ben Winthrop is another much admired leader of village opinion. An 'excellent wheelwright', he reveals village interest and pride in its music and its 'piquant' sense of humour through the 'unflinching frankness' of his insults to Mr Tookey, who cannot sing (p. 48). He is another example of parenting – devotedly proud of Aaron who 'sings like a throstle'.

Aaron Winthrop is a good example of a flat character (see Style) who remains undeveloped. He is necessary as the 'perfect young man' who will bring the 'happy ending' by marrying Eppie.

Jem Rodney as the mole catcher is ideally placed to be the local poacher – his breaking the law is socially accepted and not in the same class as William Dane and Dunstan harming Silas. He informed the other villagers of Silas's fits, increasing suspicion of him. He causes Silas to remember the pain of an unjust accusation.

Raveloe gentry *Squire Cass* is 'A tall stout man of sixty' with a 'slack and feeble mouth' and a 'hard glare', Squire Cass has an appearance of 'habitual neglect', and so has his house (p. 68). He is an inconsistent man who fails to take action when he should and then blames everyone else. He is a hard landlord, who allows Fowler to get behind with his rent and is prepared to seize his possessions. He enjoys his position in the village, 'condescending' to visit the Rainbow (p. 24), and 'patronising' his guests at New Year when he makes a great show (p. 97). The easy-going villagers disapprove that 'he had kept all his sons at home in idleness' (p. 24) and his sons fear his pride will disinherit them both (p. 26) over money and Godfrey's secret marriage. He is an example of a bad father – he neglects his sons and then becomes angry at their actions.

Make full use of George Eliot's detailed and vivid character descriptions.

Mr Lammeter is greatly admired by the villagers as a gentleman (p. 49), a father, and a farmer famous for the 'red Durham o' this countryside' (p. 46). He brought up his daughters 'that they never suffered a pinch of salt to be wasted yet everybody … had of the best' (p. 25). He was a 'grave and orderly senior' (p. 98) who would not allow his daughter to marry Godfrey before 'alteration in several ways'. He was lean and healthy, his face 'had never been flushed by excess' unlike Squire Cass whom he contrasts as a father.

Priscilla Lammeter is a 'cheerful looking lady' (p. 93). 'That excellent housewife' (p. 41) who generously gave Silas pork, her affection for her younger sister makes her agree to wear a dress which makes her 'yallow' (p. 93). Cheerfully blunt about her looks: 'I am ugly … the pretty uns do for fly-catchers – they keep the men off us' – she offends the Miss Gunns (p. 94) without noticing. She has no wish to marry and is an unusual example of a single, practical, competent woman whose 'father's a sober man and likely to live' so 'the business needn't be broken up' (p. 94).

Mr Crackenthorpe the Rector was 'not in the least lofty or aristocratic' (p. 96). He was a 'merry-eyed, small featured grey haired man' with an impressive cravat who paid Nancy complements and joined in the dancing 'as part of the fitness of things' (p. 102). 'The parson naturally set an example in these social duties' (p. 102).

George Eliot's humour makes these characters live.

Mrs Crackenthorpe the Rector's wife (p. 97) was a 'small blinking woman' who fidgeted with 'her lace, ribbons and gold chain' and made noises 'like a guinea pig'. The comical description continues when little Aaron wonders how does 'that big cock's feather stick in Mrs Crackenthorpe's yead?' (p. 103).

Doctor Kimble had followed the family tradition in becoming an apothecary. He lived very comfortably keeping 'an extravagant table' (p. 98) and employing an apprentice (p. 115). He is brother-in-law to Squire Cass, whose sister he married; they are childless (p. 118). He has lent money to his nephew Godfrey in the past. A 'thin and agile man', he is generally lively and agreeable, except when playing cards.

Mrs Kimble enjoys 'a double dignity' (p. 10) in the village as the doctor's wife and the Squire's sister. She is very fat but has 'much good humour' (p. 98) and considers her husband 'clever and amusing' (p. 100).

Mr Osgood farms at The Orchards where he entertains generously (p. 24) and his family have lived as long as the villagers can remember (p. 23). His dead sister had been the wife of Squire Cass and mother of his four sons. Mr Osgood has a son, Gilbert.

Mrs Osgood (p. 91) is elderly, rather prim, with 'curls of smooth grey hair'. 'Devoted attachment and mutual admiration' exists between her and her niece by marriage, Nancy Lammeter, although she disapproves of her niece Priscilla who was 'too rough' (p. 93). She is another of the excellent housewives in the village (p. 24).

LANGUAGE & STYLE

Try contrasting George Eliot's vocabulary, sentence and paragraph length and construction with a modern novel.

George Eliot uses full and detailed descriptions throughout the novel. A look at the choice of vocabulary, sentence and paragraph length and construction at once identify a pre-twentieth-century text. The narrator's voice vividly describes places, people, events, attitudes and atmospheres (see Literary Terms). It also uses coincidences (see Literary Terms) to briskly tell the weaver's story. These give tight control over events and economise with words.

Contrasting (see Literary Terms) actions and words highlight characters' good and bad points and form readers' opinions on them. The dialogue provides humour and brings the characters (see Literary Terms) to life, especially the Midlands dialect (see Literary Terms) and accent (from the author's childhood) used by the villagers. In contrast, the narrator uses standard English, probably to make the story easier to read than one written in dialect.

The following are important in George Eliot's style:

- Coincidence (see Literary Terms) is widely used. Probably the best example is New Year's Eve where, for example, Molly collapses outside the cottage (p. 108); Silas has a fit at his open door (p. 109); Eppie enters (p. 109); Molly dies (p. 117); and Silas decides to keep Eppie (p. 118).

- Contrast (see Literary Terms) is used often – e.g. between people (Silas and Godfrey pp. 168–9); between actions (Silas and Godfrey p. 118); between places or scenes (Raveloe p. 7 and Lantern Yard p. 15) and between atmospheres (town p. 178 and country p. 181).
- Description (see Literary Terms) – look at the sentence construction and paragraphing of the opening (p. 5). Contrast it, for example, with the details of the parlour of the Red House (p. 25) and on Nancy Lammeter (p. 92) where very clear pictures are created.

Contrast the dialogue with that of a modern novel.

- Dialogue (see Literary Terms) – look at how feelings between Godfrey and Dunstan are brought out in their quarrel (p. 25). Also look at the conversation in the Rainbow (p. 46) which reveals the period of the book and the speech patterns and accents of the villagers. The style of conversation forms a contrast to that of the gentry (p. 93) as well as a contrast to present day speech.
- Images and symbols (see Literary Terms) are used frequently, e.g. a spider (p. 16), a spinning insect (p. 17); gold (pp. 17, 21), Eppie's hair like gold (pp. 110, 181); light – Lantern Yard (note ironic name) for faith and darkness – blackness of night (p. 16) represents loss of faith and despair.
- Irony (see Literary Terms) is widely used in *Silas Marner* to great effect. For example, the narrator tells us the villagers' opinion of Godfrey (p. 24) which is ironic since he has secrets. It is dramatic irony (see Literary Terms) that the reader knows that Godfrey has a child (p. 107) but Nancy does not (p. 162).
- Narrator's voice (see Literary Terms) – the mask worn by the author to reveal thoughts, to focus

attention or comment on a person, an issue or an event. George Eliot uses the third person narrator, referring to 'he' or 'she'. Very occasionally she uses the first person (pp. 131 and 132).

- Pathetic fallacy (see Literary Terms) – look where the weather is in harmony with human actions and emotions. For example, the night Silas is robbed (p. 44) and Eppie's wedding (p. 181).

PART FOUR

STUDY SKILLS

HOW TO USE QUOTATIONS

One of the secrets of success in writing essays is the way you use quotations. There are five basic principles:

- Put inverted commas at the beginning and end of the quotation
- Write the quotation exactly as it appears in the original
- Do not use a quotation that repeats what you have just written
- Use the quotation so that it fits into your sentence
- Keep the quotation as short as possible

Quotations should be used to develop the line of thought in your essays.

Your comment should not duplicate what is in your quotation. For example:

> **The narrator tells us that the story of the linen-weaver, Silas Marner, begins in the early years of the nineteenth century through the quotation 'in the early years of this century'.**

Far more effective is to write:

> **The narrator tells us that Silas Marner's story begins 'in the early years of this century.**

However, the most sophisticated way of using the writer's words is to embed them into your sentence:

> **The narrator reveals a linen-weaver named Silas Marner, worked at his vocation in the backward-looking village of Raveloe 'quite an hour's journey on horseback from any turnpike'.**

When you use quotations in this way, you are demonstrating the ability to use text as evidence to support your ideas - not simply including words from the original to prove you have read it.

Everyone writes differently. Work through the suggestions given here and adapt the advice to suit your own style and interests. This will improve your essay-writing skills and allow your personal voice to emerge.

The following points indicate in ascending order the skills of essay writing:

- Picking out one or two facts about the story and adding the odd detail
- Writing about the text by retelling the story
- Retelling the story and adding a quotation here and there
- Organising an answer which explains what is happening in the text and giving quotations to support what you write

....

- Writing in such a way as to show that you have thought about the intentions of the writer of the text and that you understand the techniques used
- Writing at some length, giving your viewpoint on the text and commenting by picking out details to support your views
- Looking at the text as a work of art, demonstrating clear critical judgement and explaining to the reader of your essay how the enjoyment of the text is assisted by literary devices, linguistic effects and psychological insights; showing how the text relates to the time when it was written

The dotted line above represents the division between lower and higher level grades. Higher-level performance begins when you start to consider your response as a reader of the text. The highest level is reached when you offer an enthusiastic personal response and show how this piece of literature is a product of its time.

Coursework essay

Set aside an hour or so at the start of your to work plan what you have to do.

- List all the points you feel are needed to cover the task. Collect page references of information and quotations that will support what you have to say. A helpful tool is the highlighter pen: this saves painstaking copying and enables you to target precisely what you want to use.
- Focus on what you consider to be the main points of the essay. Try to sum up your argument in a single sentence, which could be the closing sentence of your essay. Depending on the essay title, it could be a statement about a character: The theft of his gold could have made Silas Marner more bitter and isolated. Instead he accepts responsibility for Eppie and becomes a happier person, accepted and admired by the Raveloe community; an opinion about setting: I think Raveloe represents a threatened community in a changing world. George Eliot believed country values were lost through the economic and social changes brought by the Industrial Revolution and world events; or a judgement on a theme: I think justice is the main theme in *Silas Marner* because, in the end, the characters who choose to do good are rewarded but those who neglect their duty or choose to do ill are punished.
- Make a short essay plan. Use the first paragraph to introduce the argument you wish to make. In the following paragraphs develop this argument with details, examples and other possible points of view. Sum up your argument in the last paragraph. Check you have answered the question.
- Write the essay, remembering all the time the central point you are making.
- On completion, go back over what you have written to eliminate careless errors and improve expression. Read it aloud to yourself, or, if you

are feeling more confident, to a relative or friend.

If you can, try to type your essay using a word processor. This will allow you to correct and improve your writing without spoiling its appearance.

Examination essay

The essay written in an examination often carries more marks than the coursework essay even though it is written under considerable time pressure.

In the revision period build up notes on various aspects of the text you are using. Fortunately, in acquiring this set of York Notes on *Silas Marner*, you have made a prudent beginning! York Notes are set out to give you vital information and help you to construct your personal overview of the text.

Make notes with appropriate quotations about the key issues of the set text. Go into the examination knowing your text and having a clear set of opinions about it.

In most English Literature examinations you can take in copies of your set books. This in an enormous advantage although it may lull you into a false sense of security. Beware! There is simply not enough time in an examination to read the book from scratch.

In the examination

- Read the question paper carefully and remind yourself what you have to do.
- Look at the questions on your set texts to select the one that most interests you and mentally work out the points you wish to stress.
- Remind yourself of the time available and how you are going to use it.
- Briefly map out a short plan in note form that will keep your writing on track and illustrate the key argument you want to make.
- Then set about writing it.
- When you have finished, check through to eliminate errors.

To summarise, these are the keys to success

- **Know the text**
- **Have a clear understanding of and opinions on the storyline, characters, setting, themes and writer's concerns**
- **Select the right material**
- **Plan and write a clear response, continually bearing the question in mind**

SAMPLE ESSAY PLAN

A typical essay question on *Silas Marner* is followed by a sample essay plan in note form. This does not present the only answer to the question, merely one answer. Do not be afraid to include your own ideas and leave out some of the ones in this sample! Remember that quotations are essential to prove and illustrate the points you make.

In your opinion who made the best father: Squire Cass, his son Godfrey, or Silas Marner? How did George Eliot influence your choice?

Part 1

Introduce your subject by explaining what you would look for in a good father. For example, his personality, circumstances, what he says and does, his motives, the opinions other characters have of him and his relationship with his child or children.

Part 2

Develop the subject by considering each of the fathers: compare and contrast them. Remember to include supporting evidence through short quotations, ideally only two or three words long, whenever possible. Identify the skills George Eliot used to reveal her characters and how this influences your choice. You could use:

- Description (see Literary Terms) – the personality of each character and appearance if relevant
- Use of narrator's voice (see Literary Terms) and any other use of language features

- Use of coincidence (see Literary Terms); other features of plot (see Literary Terms)
- Use of irony (see Literary Terms)
- Use of contrast (see Literary Terms)
- Use of symbols or imagery (see Literary Terms)
- Use of atmosphere (see Literary Terms)

Explain your understanding of George Eliot's purpose in using these skills.

Part 3 Conclude by measuring each character against your list for an ideal father. Name and explain your choice of best, second best, and worst father.

FURTHER QUESTIONS

1. The good are rewarded and the bad are punished – is *Silas Marner* a moral tale?
2. Compare and contrast two novels of your own choice, one from the nineteenth and one from the twentieth centuries. Use your understanding of the social, historical and cultural backgrounds of each to explain which you enjoyed most.
3. What part do injustice and misunderstanding play in the life of Silas Marner?
4. After reading the text of *Silas Marner* and watching the video, which version do you prefer? Explain your reasons for your choice. (To do this essay, you need to be aware of all changes and differences from the original text and their effects.)

Part five

Cultural connections

Broader perspectives

Film and video versions

You can increase your understanding and enjoyment of *Silas Marner* through dramatisations such as the BBC video version (THE 20041), starring Ben Kingsley. These versions help you to:

- Visualise period and place
- Understand the importance of period and place to plot
- Understand what themes or issues may be important in period or place
- Understand the characters and actions arising from period and place – people and environment

This is an easy and pleasant way of absorbing many important details.

Relationship to other texts

If you have enjoyed George Eliot's short, simple *Silas Marner*, an interesting follow-on would be to read her longer, more complex *Middlemarch* (Penguin Classics, 1994 – first published 1871). This is often considered her best novel and like *Silas Marner* is set in a country environment in the first half of the nineteenth century. This is also available as a BBC video (1994).

A different way to examine the novel's broader perspective would be to compare and contrast it with a novel set in a different period and place, e.g. Harper Lee's *To Kill a Mockingbird* (Minerva, 1991) covers many of the issues raised in *Silas Marner*.

LITERARY TERMS

allusion a reference which briefly recalls something in another text
atmosphere mood – varies according to what is said or done
character the imaginary people in a book also their personalities as revealed by descriptions by what they say and do; or others say about them
coincidence artificial unrealistic organisation of time and place of events to suit plot
context events before and after an incident in the book
contrast when opposites are introduced to balance or highlight characters, places, events or issues
description using words to create scenes, objects, people, behaviour, attitudes and atmosphere
dialect the special words and style of speaking particular to an area or region
dialogue speech and conversation used by the book's characters
dramatic irony when the plot allows the readers of a book to know more than some of the characters in the book
imagery means use of metaphors and similes; also means use of objects to rouse feelings
irony speaking or writing one thing while really meaning another. It includes sarcasm
metaphor the writer states that one thing is another. There is no intention to deceive and is intended to arouse the imagination
narrator's voice this is not the personal opinion of the author, but a mechanism or mask used to tell the story. Can be first person; speaking through 'I' or 'we'. Can be third person; refers to 'he', 'she', 'they' etc
pathetic fallacy when a writer emphasises a character's mood by linking it to the surrounding world. This is often done through nature and natural events such as weather, but can be man-made
personification to give human qualities to an animal or object
plot organisation of the events in a book
sarcasm an ironic speech which mocks, taunts or insults the person spoken to; but amuses onlookers
setting time (period) and place where the events of the novel take place. Can be used to reveal characters and atmospheres
simile figure of speech which compares unlikely objects or people through shared characteristics: uses 'like' or 'as'
symbol one thing is used to represent another

Test answers

Test yourself (Chapters 1–3)

A...
1 The narrator *(Chapter 1)*
2 Mr Macey *(Chapter 1)*
3 Silas Marner *(Chapter 1)*
4 Godfrey Cass *(Chapter 3)*
5 Squire Cass *(Chapter 3)*
6 William Dane *(Chapter 1)*
7 Dunstan Cass *(Chapter 3)*

Test yourself (Chapters 4–10)

A...
1 Mr Snell *(Chapter 7)*
2 Jem Rodney *(Chapter 7)*
3 Mr Dowlas *(Chapter 7)*
4 Squire Cass *(Chapter 9)*
5 Dunstan Cass *(Chapter 4)*
6 Aaron Winthrop *(Chapter 6)*
7 Mr Crackenthorpe *(Chapter 10)*

Test yourself (Chapters 11–15)

A...
1 Priscilla Lammeter *(Chapter 11)*
2 Doctor Kimble *(Chapter 11)*
3 Ben Winthrop *(Chapter 11)*
4 Nancy Lammeter *(Chapter 11)*
5 Nancy Lammeter *(Chapter 11)*
6 Mr Lammeter *(Chapter 11)*
7 Molly Farren *(Chapter 12)*

Test yourself (Chapters 16–18)

A...
1 Silas Marner *(Chapter 16)*
2 Dolly Winthrop *(Chapter 16)*
3 Priscilla Lammeter *(Chapter 17)*
4 Silas Marner *(Chapter 16)*
5 Godfrey Cass *(Chapter 18)*
6 Godfrey Cass *(Chapter 16)*
7 Nancy Lammeter *(Chapter 17)*

Test yourself (Chapter 19–Conclusion)

A...
1 Eppie *(Chapter 19)*
2 Godfrey Cass *(Chapter 19)*
3 Dolly Winthrop *(Chapter 21)*
4 Mr Macey *(Conclusion)*
5 Silas Marner *(Chapter 19)*
6 Nancy Lammeter *(Conclusion)*
7 Silas Marner *(Conclusion)*

MAP OF RAVELOE

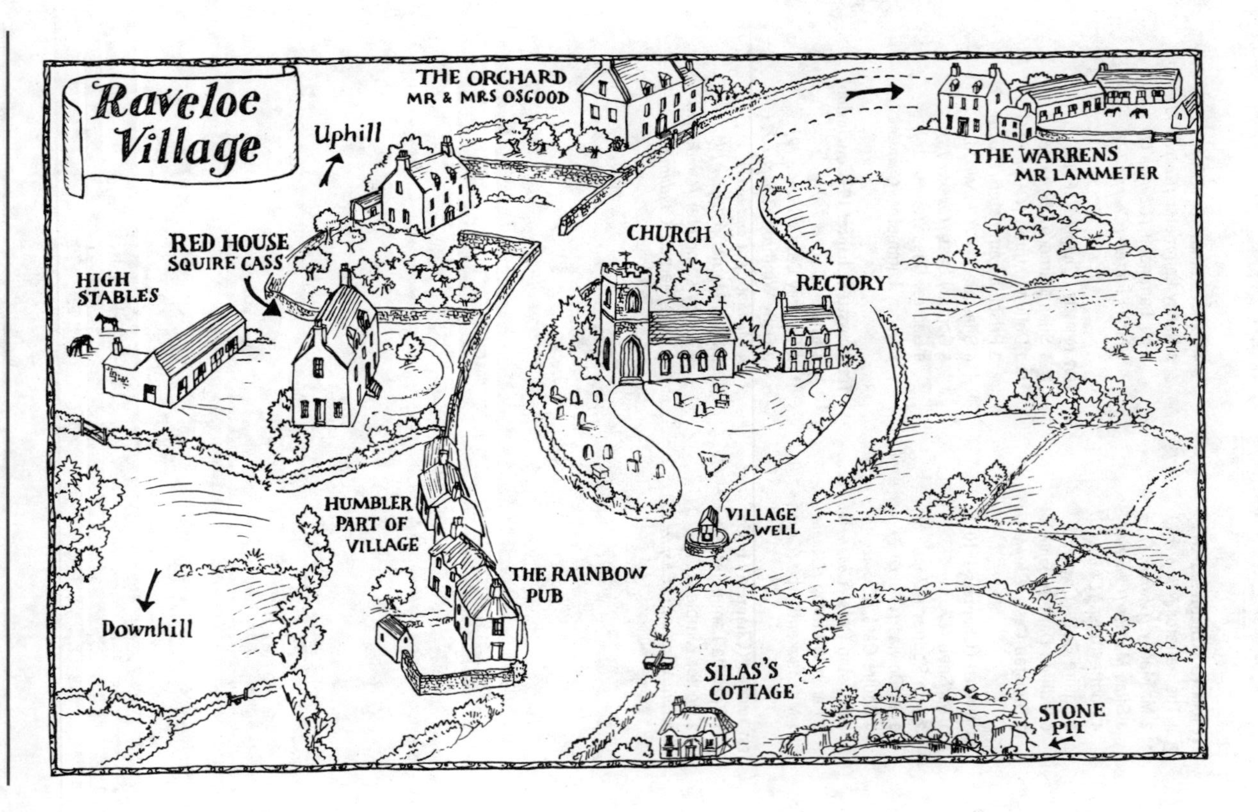